Integrating Total Quality Management in a Library Setting

Integrating Total Quality Management in a Library Setting

Susan Jurow
Susan B. Barnard
Editors

The Haworth Press, Inc.
New York • London • Norwood (Australia)

Integrating Total Quality Management in a Library Setting has also been published as *Journal of Library Administration*, Volume 18, Numbers 1/2 1993.

The Haworth Press, Inc., 10 Alice Street, Binghamton, NY 13904-1580, USA

Library of Congress Cataloging-in-Publication Data

Integrating total quality management in a library setting / Susan Jurow, Susan B. Barnard, editors.
      p. cm.
      Includes bibliographical references and index.
      ISBN 1-56024-463-1 (acid free paper).–ISBN 1-56024-464-X (pbk. : acid free paper)
      1. Library administration–United States. 2. Total quality management–United States.
I. Jurow, Susan. II. Barnard, Susan B.
Z678.I56 1993
025.1'0973–dc20
                                                     93-12942
                                                         CIP

INDEXING & ABSTRACTING

Contributions to this publication are selectively indexed or abstracted in print, electronic, online, or CD-ROM version(s) of the reference tools and information services listed below. This list is current as of the copyright date of this publication. See the end of this section for additional notes.

- *Academic Abstracts/CD-ROM,* EBSCO, Publishing, P.O. Box 2250, Peabody, MA 01960-7250

- *AGRICOLA Database,* National Agricultural Library, 10301 Baltimore Boulevard, Room 002, Beltsville, MD 20705

- *Bulletin Signaletique,* INIST/CNRS-Service Gestion des Documents Primaires, 2, allee du Parc de Brabois, F-54514 Vandoeuvre-les-Nancy, Cedex, France

- *Cambridge Scientific Abstracts, Health & Safety Science Abstracts,* Cambridge Information Group, 7200 Wisconsin Avenue #601, Bethesda, MD 20814

- *Current Articles on Library Literature and Services (CALLS),* Pakistan Library Association, Quaid-e-Azam Library, Bagh-e-Jinnah, Lahore, Pakistan

- *Current Awareness Bulletin,* Association for Information Management, Information House, 20-24 Old Street, London EC1V 9AP, England

- *Current Index to Journals in Education,* Syracuse University, 030 Huntington Hall, Syracuse, NY 13244-2340

- *Educational Administration Abstracts,* Sage Publications, Inc., 2455 Teller Road, Newbury Park, CA 91320

- *Foreign Library and Information Service,* China Sci-Tech Book Review, Library of Academia Sinica, 8 Kexueyuan Nanlu, Zhongguancun, Beijing 100080, People's Republic of China

(continued)

- **Higher Education Abstracts,** Claremont Graduate School, 740 North College Avenue, Claremont, CA 91711

- **Index to Periodical Articles Related to Law,** University of Texas, 727 East 26th Street, Austin, TX 78705

- **Information Reports & Bibliographies,** Science Associates International, Inc., 465 West End Avenue, New York, NY 10024

- **Information Science Abstracts,** Plenum Publishing Company, 233 Spring Street, New York, NY 10013-1578

- **INSPEC Information Services,** Institution of Electrical Engineers, Michael Faraday House, Six Hills Way, Stevenage, Herts SG1 2AY, England

- **Library & Information Science Abstracts (LISA),** Bowker-Saur Limited, 60 Grosvenor Street, London W1X 9DA, England

- **Library Literature,** The H.W. Wilson Company, 950 University Avenue, Bronx, NY 10452

- **OT BibSys,** American Occupational Therapy Foundation, P.O. Box 1725, Rockville, MD 20849-1725

- **Public Affairs Information Bulletin (PAIS),** Public Affairs Information Service, Inc., 521 West 43rd Street, New York, NY 10036-4396

- **Referativnyi Zhurnal (Abstracts Journal of the Institute of Scientific Information of the Republic of Russia),** The Institute of Scientific Information, Baltijskaja ul., 14, Moscow A-219, Republic of Russia

- **Trade & Industry Index,** Information Access Company, 362 Lakeside Drive, Foster City, CA 94404

- **Women in Management Review Abstracts,** Anbar Abstracts, 62 Toller Lane, Bradford, West Yorkshire BD8 9BY, England

Book reviews are selectively excerpted by the *Guide to Professional Literature of the Journal of Academic Librarianship.*

(continued)

SPECIAL BIBLIOGRAPHIC NOTES

related to indexing and abstracting

☐ indexing/abstracting services in this list will also cover material in the "separate" that is co-published simultaneously with Haworth's special thematic journal issue or DocuSerial. Indexing/abstracting usually covers material at the article/chapter level.

☐ monographic co-editions are intended for either non-subscribers or libraries which intend to purchase a second copy for their circulating collections.

☐ monographic co-editions are reported to all jobbers/wholesalers/approval plans. The source journal is listed as the "series" to assist the prevention of duplicate purchasing in the same manner utilized for books-in-series.

☐ to facilitate user/access services all indexing/abstracting services are encouraged to utilize the co-indexing entry note indicated at the bottom of the first page of each article/chapter/contribution.

☐ this is intended to assist a library user of any reference tool (whether print, electronic, online, or CD-ROM) to locate the monographic version if the library has purchased this version but not a subscription to the source journal.

☐ individual articles/chapters in any Haworth publication are also available through the Haworth Document Delivery Services (HDDS).

Integrating Total Quality Management in a Library Setting

CONTENTS

ABOUT THE EDITORS

Susan Jurow is Director of the Association of Research Libraries, Office of Management Services (OMS). She has worked at OMS for eight years, serving as Program Officer for Training and Associate Director before becoming the Director in 1990. Ms. Jurow is responsible for overall direction for the Office and provides training and consulting in public services operations and library management. She received her B.A. from Stanford University in French and an M.L.S. from Rutgers University. She has held public services and administrative positions at Stanford University, the University of Houston, and the University of California.

Susan B. Barnard is Head of Periodical Information and Access Services (PIAS) at the Kent State University Libraries. She has a B.A. degree from Stetson University, an M.L.S. degree from Kent State University, and an M.A. in American Studies from Case Western Reserve University. Her previous positions include Assistant to the Dean of University Libraries and Media Services, and Reference Librarian at Kent State University, and Assistant Librarian, Congressional Quarterly/Editorial Research Reports Library, Washington, D.C. During 1991/92 while on sabbatical leave from Kent State University, she served as Visiting Program Officer at the Association of Research Libraries' Office of Management Services, where she worked on applications of total quality management in university and research library settings.

Introduction:
TQM Fundamentals
and Overview of Contents

Susan Jurow
Susan B. Barnard

A great deal has been written about Total Quality Management (TQM); books, articles, pamphlets, and handbooks describe the basic principles, the process, useful techniques, the advantages and disadvantages, who the leading experts are, and "how we done it good." To date very little of it has related directly or indirectly to libraries. TQM was developed in a manufacturing environment, and the process of translating it to a service environment has been a slow one. In addition, many of those who work in libraries differentiate between their not-for-profit service arena and for-profit service operations, and they are slow to embrace techniques and attitudes from the for-profit sector.

In this volume, we have brought together people who have begun to think about using or who are already using TQM in a library setting. The articles examine both planning and implementation issues. We also included articles that describe programs outside of libraries that we feel would support efforts to implement TQM

[Haworth co-indexing entry note]: "Introduction: TQM Fundamentals and Overview of Contents." Jurow, Susan, and Susan B. Barnard. Co-published simultaneously in the *Journal of Library Administration*, (The Haworth Press, Inc.) Vol. 18, No. 1/2, 1993, pp. 1-13; and: *Integrating Total Quality Management in a Library Setting* (ed: Susan Jurow, and Susan B. Barnard), The Haworth Press, Inc., 1993, pp. 1-13. Multiple copies of this article/chapter may be purchased from The Haworth Document Delivery Center. Call 1-800-3-HA-WORTH (1-800-342-9678) between 9:00 - 5:00 (EST) and ask for DOCUMENT DELIVERY CENTER.

within libraries. Because we believe that there is much to learn from the experience of others, we also contacted people who work in other non-manufacturing settings to comment on how TQM has been engaged in their fields.

We begin with a discussion of what TQM is, where it comes from, and the potential benefits and barriers we might expect to experience in adopting quality approaches in libraries.

WHAT IS TOTAL QUALITY MANAGEMENT?

In 1954 John Foster Dulles, Secretary of State, said, "Japan will never produce anything that American consumers will want to buy." By 1990 the U.S. had lost 40% of its market share to foreign competitors while Japan had increased its foreign market by 500%; fifty of the world's 100 largest companies were Japanese, and there were no American-made VCR's, compact disc players or single-lens reflex cameras.

The landmark work of an American statistician and management theorist, Dr. W. Edwards Deming, with Japanese manufacturers following World War II is credited with helping Japan to dramatically improve the quality of its products and achieve a commanding world economic position. The "quality revolution" in American management during the last twenty years also is traceable to the Japanese principles advanced by Dr. Deming. Deming's principles, summarized in his fourteen points for management, have been adopted by hundreds of U.S. companies, including Federal Express, Ford Motor Company, Xerox, IBM, Hewlett-Packard, Westinghouse, Corning, Motorola and many others. A 1990 survey found that about fifty percent of *Business Week*'s 1000 top companies had initiated a quality improvement program of some type. Firmly established in business and industry, TQM is now being embraced in government, the military, education and other non-profit sectors of the U.S.

Total quality management as practiced today combines theories, models and tools developed by Dr. Deming and fellow "quality gurus" Joseph Juran and Philip Crosby, and applied in U.S. and foreign industries. Simply defined, TQM is "a system of continuous improvement employing participative management and centered on the needs of customers." Hallmarks of TQM include employee involvement and training; problem-solving teams; statistical methods; long-term goals and thinking; and recognition that the system (not employees) is responsible for most inefficiencies.

Can TQM, a system designed for and successfully applied in business and manufacturing settings, be effectively employed in non-profit, service organizations, such as libraries? Deming says his principles apply to any business, education or government, wherever an organization must stay ahead of its customers. In fact, TQM embodies certain values and approaches common to research libraries today, yet several of its defining and most extraordinary elements—continuous improvement, quality tools and measurement, and customer-focused planning—are not commonly applied in libraries.

In applying total quality methods in libraries, consideration should be given to the benefits, as well as potential barriers, likely to be realized or encountered.

BENEFITS OF TQM IN LIBRARIES

While TQM offers many obvious benefits to libraries, there are a few fundamental concepts of TQM which merit special attention. These are concepts largely unfamiliar to libraries but which seem to have strong potential to offer new insights and strategies in library management. They are: breaking down interdepartmental barriers, the internal customer, and continuous improvement.

Breaking down interdepartmental barriers. Like other complex, highly structured and basically hierarchical organizations, libraries tend to divide staff and functions into specialized units responsible for discrete aspects of the library's overall mission of providing information resources, or access to resources, for its users. By working together on problem-solving teams, established to address specific operational questions, and by developing a shared knowledge of problem-solving tools and techniques, staff not only grow personally; they learn about and participate in issues affecting other departments and gain a larger sense of organizational purpose.

The concept of the internal customer. By redefining the beneficiaries of library services and work processes as "internal and external customers," a different perspective can be gained as to the purpose of these processes, and possible ways of changing, improving or eliminating them. The concept of the internal customer is a particularly powerful one for libraries. Internal customers are people inside the organization who receive the output of the organization's processes–whether it be goods, information, or services–and use it in their own work. In most cases there are both immediate internal customers and internal customers further down the line who are affected by the process. Four key questions help to define internal customer requirements:

- What do you need from me?
- What do you do with what I give you?
- Is there any gap between what you need and what I give to you?
- Is there anything I'm giving you that you don't need?

These questions and the dialogue they create allow analysis of work processes and practices from an interdepartmental perspective, and promote broader understanding of activities performed, and how they contribute to meeting customer needs, throughout the library.

Continuous improvement. Continuous improvement is not defined as trying to do better all the time (What organization isn't or doesn't believe that it is doing this?) Traditional management approaches often focus on maintaining the status quo with the familiar motto, "If it ain't broke, don't fix it." The TQM approach shifts focus to continuous improvement in systems and processes. Its motto could be "Continue to improve it even if it ain't broke."

Continuous improvement uses specific methods and measurements to systematically collect and analyze data for the purpose of improving the processes identified as critical to the organization's mission. The components of continuous improvement are both a philosophy and a set of graphical problem-solving tools or techniques: examples of these are brainstorming, the flowchart, Pareto chart, control chart, and scatter diagram. Graphical techniques can show an organization how its processes work, what its baselines are, where the variations lie, the relative importance of problems to be solved, and whether changes made have had the desired impact.

Continuous improvement rests on the simple premise that a structured, problem-solving process produces better results than an unstructured one. Instead of just trying to "do better" in an undefined, intuitive way, continuous improvement can enable libraries to set measurable goals, based on quantitative performance indicators, and to monitor progress toward those goals.

BARRIERS TO ADOPTION OF TQM IN LIBRARIES

The vocabulary barrier. Initial objections voiced by librarians and academics alike, when introduced to the principles of TQM, are usually over its specialized vocabulary, derived from and still closely associated with business and the marketplace. The words "total," "quality" and "management" themselves all seem to send up red flags in academic and service environments. Promoting "quality" principles seems, on the surface, to imply that standards are not already being observed nor quality work, valued. And referring to students as "customers" is sure to prompt protestations from faculty to the effect that universities are not in the "business" of "selling" learning and knowledge.

As Karyle Butcher points out in her article about adopting TQM at the Oregon State University Library, arguments about the language of TQM are time-consuming and may never be resolved. But, since most would agree that inventing a new vocabulary is not a worthwhile endeavor, it's probably best to limit the discussion of terminology and focus, instead, on the principles, strategies and benefits of TQM.

The commitment barrier. Several articles in this collection emphasize that TQM is not a quick fix; it requires long-term commitment, perhaps even longer in the service sector (three to five years to implement) than in the private sector. This is because new models must be created and new territory, charted. Fortunately, in the service sector, the longevity of managers is not as precarious as it is in many industries. For example, in the auto manufacturing industry, a chief executive may be dismissed for a single unprofitable year. Yet, turnover among both university and library officials is relatively high. And library managers, particularly in times of financial duress, may seek short-term solutions and dramatic turnarounds.

These managers may be reluctant to undertake a TQM transition, or to be discouraged when quick results do not occur. TQM is about fundamental, cultural change which cannot be accomplished overnight, or in a year, though positive changes, particularly in staff attitudes and learning, should occur early in the process.

The process barrier. As Constance Towler points out in her article in this volume, we have been trained as a culture to try to solve problems quickly and then get on to something else. We tend to be impatient with process and eager for closure, as if process merely represents a desire to postpone decision making or reluctance to resolve an issue. Consequently, we often rush to the fastest solution and then later have to solve the same or related problems that result from our partial solutions. Instead, we may need to learn to define problems better at the outset and then give them the kind of systematic analysis which can lead to lasting solutions. TQM processes and its focus on process analysis can help in this.

The professionalization barrier. The higher the degree of professionalization within an organization, the greater the resistance to certain elements of TQM, particularly its customer focus. Professionals simply are mystified by, if not fearful of, the consequences of what they think could mean turning over their services and practices, which are based on tradition, standards and respected bodies of knowledge, to the uninformed whims of customers.

For example, an area where TQM has had a very substantial impact beyond the manufacturing sector, is in the health care field. Hospital accrediting agencies in both the U.S. and Canada are moving to require that hospitals practice continuous improvement in order to achieve full accreditation. However, in hospitals it is usually the doctors who are least amenable to the kinds of changes in perspective and practice which TQM inspires. In universities, TQM efforts usually begin in non-academic, support service areas such as finance, facilities, maintenance, and computer services. When Texas Instruments began to bring customer requirements and needs into circuit-breaker design, a prevailing attitude among the engineers was, "No one knows more about circuit-breakers than TI. The customers ought to be listening to us."[1] It isn't difficult to imagine that same attitude being voiced in libraries.

OVERVIEW OF CONTENTS

Section One: Library Approaches
to Total Quality Management

The first article examines TQM from a library director's perspective. Written by Kaye Gapen, Director of the University Library at Case Western Reserve University, with an organizational development consultant and a library staff member, it focuses on the reasons that a library administrator would consider using TQM as a management tool. It links the need to consider radically rethinking the way in which a library is organized and performs its functions with the turbulent, rapidly changing nature of the information environment in which libraries operate. With its emphasis on meeting user needs, TQM is seen as a way of linking the familiar, time-honored commitment to service with a flexible, future-oriented approach to management.

The second article, written by Mary Beth Clack, Staff Development Officer and Serial Records Librarian at Harvard College Library, draws a connection between TQM and strategic planning, and between TQM and organizational development. In describing the elements of the process undertaken in her library, Ms. Clack's article suggests the kinds of issues that must be considered to adequately prepare staff for a TQM effort.

Karyle Butcher, Assistant University Librarian for Research and Public Services, Oregon State University's Kerr Library, writes about her library's experience with the implementation of TQM. She provides the background to the decision to use TQM and describes two pilot projects. As might be expected, the efforts had both benefits and drawbacks. The lessons learned from this experience are easily transferable to other library situations.

Drawing on sources in business and the higher education community, Susan Barnard presents a model for the implementation of TQM in a library setting. It outlines a ten-step process divided into four stages. The approach is a flexible one that can be applied in different ways to a variety of situations depending on the level of support for implementing TQM both within and outside of the library.

Section Two: Implementing a Total Quality Management Program

A focus on the customer is clearly at the center of the TQM philosophy. However, as has been discussed, use of the word "customer" is controversial in library circles, as is the term "customer service." Here again is a vocabulary barrier that may be preventing those who work in libraries from being open to approaches that could improve library service and increase patron satisfaction. Arlene Farber Sirkin has brought together her background in business with her library background to pose some interesting questions for her library colleagues about the way they view their interactions with the public.

In reading the TQM literature, it is clear that training is a key component, and almost all the articles in this collection touch on it in one form or another. At each stage in the implementation of TQM, a different set of skills is required of staff. Some of the skills may be completely new; many, however, are skills that we have always "expected" staff to have, but for which they have never been trained. The implementation of TQM provides a library organization with the opportunity to update and enhance the abilities of the staff to work effectively and to work effectively together.

The next two articles focus specifically on training, presenting it from two different perspectives. The first, by Tim Loney and Arnie Bellefontaine, both with the U.S. General Services Administration, matches the steps in the TQM implementation process with the appropriate training effort. It emphasizes the need to recognize customer relations as a critical component in the work of library staff and as a set of skills for which people should be trained. This article also highlights the importance of training at the senior management level in the TQM process.

Meeting management and problem-solving are examples of the kinds of skills "expected" of staff, but for which training is seldom provided. Connie Towler's article speaks directly to the issue of problem-solving. An organizational culture that values continuous improvement is one of the most important goals of TQM. To ensure the successful integration of TQM into a library's management approach, staff need to understand how to think analytically, how to recognize and fix problems, and how to use measurement as a tool for improvement, rather than as an evaluative mechanism for apportioning blame. Ms. Towler's article outlines the kind of program and the kinds of skills that would support this approach.

Susan Jurow's article builds on Ms. Towler's article by providing an overview of the kinds of techniques and tools available for the systematic investigation of problems. In the process of continuous improvement, library staff must build skills in using analytical tools that provide data that can be used to understand and solve problems. She outlines the steps in a benchmarking process, a powerful approach to establishing levels of excellence.

Section Three: Supporting Total Quality Management Efforts

One of the questions we asked ourselves in outlining this volume was what kinds of external support manufacturing companies and others had to leverage their efforts to fully engage TQM within their economic sectors. The Federal government's Baldrige award was clearly an inducement. It not only set high standards that were a challenge to meet, but it also required winners to open their processes to others as models, and demanded they require their business partners to engage in the same practices. Partnerships and standards seem to be part of the formula for encouraging the use of TQM.

In his article, David Penniman, President of the Council on Library Resources, challenges the library community to make a commitment to developing the means for measuring quality operations and services in libraries. Using the Federal government's Baldrige award as a model, he outlines the benefits and rewards of such an approach for both individual libraries and the profession as a whole, and he offers to help establish a similar award within the library community.

The next article is by Richard Lynch, Lois Bacon and Ted Barnes who all work for the Faxon Company, an organization well-known for the services it provides to libraries and information management centers. They provide an example of the kinds of partnerships libraries could expect to develop with their vendors. Their approach encourages us to see libraries as part of a much larger service system, thereby expanding the options available for improving service to our patrons.

Section Four: Learning from the Experience of Others

The last three articles provide an overview of efforts being made in other arenas. Maureen Sullivan and Jack Siggins have outlined the major efforts currently underway in the higher education community. Robyn Frank and Gene Matysek provide insight into the use of TQM in the Federal government setting. Ms. Frank's article is a history and overview of the integration of TQM into the Federal bureaucracy. Mr. Matysek reports on the implementation of TQM in one agency and provides useful information about the benefits and pitfalls of large-scale projects of this nature.

CONCLUSION

This collection is a snapshot of a dynamic process. From discussion with colleagues in our informal network, it is clear that many libraries are beginning to experiment with TQM, selectively trying out the techniques and processes that seem most applicable. It is our belief that as librarians and library staff become familiar with the concepts underlying TQM, they will come to appreciate the similarities between the traditional service attitude of libraries and the customer service focus of TQM.

An IBM Vice-President said, "Nowhere is quality more critical than in organizations and institutions involved in handling information." He characterized IBM as a company moving from the "information technology" business to the "information solutions" business.[2] Perhaps libraries should incorporate this view into their own visions for the 21st century.

TQM RESOURCES

The following, highly selective list contains TQM resources (organizations, associations and suppliers) which the editors believe to be among the best sources of additional TQM information, materials and professional contacts for educators and librarians.

American Productivity and Quality Center
123 North Post Oak Lane
Houston, TX 77024-7797

Seeks to improve productivity and the quality of work life in the U.S. by working with businesses, unions, academics and government. Concentrates on productivity and quality management, productivity measurement, quality improvement, labor/management relations, and employee involvement. Maintains a library and the International Benchmarking Clearinghouse. Sponsors are corporations, foundations and individuals.

American Society for Training and Development (ASTD)
TQM Network
1630 Duke Street
Box 1443
Alexandria, VA 22313

One of the fastest-growing sections of ASTD, the TQM Network grew from 75 people to 1500 in its first 18 months of existence (Spring 1990 to Fall 1991). Open to members of ASTD, it serves as the primary linkage point within ASTD for the exploration of TQM; provides information and resources to its members as well as to ASTD as a whole; publishes a member newsletter, conducts surveys, and compiles lists of resources.

Association for Quality and Participation (AQP)
801–B West 8th Street
Cincinnati, OH 45203

A not-for-profit organization dedicated to helping organizations reach higher levels of quality through greater employee involvement and participation; "Professional Education Series" offers over 80 courses on variety of topics; "AQP Information Center"–a clearinghouse on participation information and quality techniques from around the world. Has an annual conference and publishes *The*

Journal for Quality and Participation and the *AQP Report* and an extensive resource catalog. Membership–$75.00/year for individuals with group and team discounts.

Federal Quality Institute
(U.S. Office of Personnel Management)
Box 99
Washington, DC 20044-0099

Established in 1988 to promote and facilitate the implementation of TQM throughout the Federal government. Its three-fold mission is (1) to provide quality awareness training to Federal government managers; (2) to provide private-sector quality experts whom Federal agencies can use to assist in the implementation of TQM; and (3) to maintain the Quality and Productivity Resource Information Center, a library with materials on quality practices and training. More important to non-federal libraries is its *Federal Total Quality Management Handbook*, an excellent series of published and forthcoming booklets (available as U.S. Depository items) each addressing a major area of Total Quality Management implementation, including *Introduction to Total Quality Management in the Federal Government*, *How to Get Started*, and *Criteria and Scoring Guidelines for the President's Award for Quality and Productivity Improvement*.

Films Incorporated
5547 Ravenswood Avenue
Chicago, Illinois 60640-1199

Issues an annual "Total Quality" catalog of training videos on all aspects of quality management and related subjects, including change, teamwork, communication, partnerships, performance appraisal, etc.

GOAL/QPC
13 Branch Street
Methuen, MA 01844-1953

Founded in 1978, GOAL/QPC is a nonprofit organization specializing in understanding TQM as it is practiced around the world.

Offers "leading edge" research, educational and training courses, consulting and publications on TQM. While early emphasis of the organization was on business sector applications, growing areas of emphasis are on government, health care and education, each of which has a network within the organization. Annual conference each Fall in Boston now has an educational track. Send for its *Customer Guide* which describes the organization and its programs. Individual membership: $50.00/year.

National Educational Quality Initiative, Inc. (NEQI)
P.O Box 13
Cedarburg, WI 53012

An effort of the American Society for Quality Control (ASQC) and the Federal Interagency Committee on Education (FICE), co-sponsors of the first National Educational Quality Initiative seminar in May 1988, to coordinate national consideration of issues of quality that affect education. Now a Wisconsin non-profit membership corporation whose purpose it is to foster three ambitious objectives: (1) to obtain inclusion of appropriate portions of quality sciences and associated arts into all educational courses in the U.S.; (2) to incorporate quality science and associated arts into all aspects of educational administration; (3) to improve the quality of content and delivery of all material in the entire educational process. Three categories of membership: Corporate, Academic (Educator–$35.00; Student–$15.00), and Individual ($50.00 and $75.00).

NOTES

1. Address by William Polleys, former President of Texas Instruments Materials Control Group at the GOAL/QPC Annual Conference, Boston, MA, November 11, 1991

2. Address by Stephen Schwarz, Vice President for Market-Driven Quality at IBM, at the GOAL/QPC Annual Conference, Boston, MA, November 12, 1991.

LIBRARY APPROACHES TO TOTAL QUALITY MANAGEMENT

TQM:
The Director's Perspective

D. Kaye Gapen
Queen Hampton
Sharon Schmitt

WHY CONSIDER TQM?

Perhaps the first question to ask, after one understands what TQM as a management methodology consists of, is "Why TQM?" For that matter, why would any library director explore organiza-

D. Kaye Gapen is Director of University Libraries at Case Western Reserve University, Cleveland, OH. Queen Hampton is an External Consultant throughout northeastern Ohio and serves as Manager of Information Resources. Sharon Schmitt is Assistant to the Director of University Libraries at Case Western Reserve University.

[Haworth co-indexing entry note]: "TQM: The Director's Perspective." Gapen, D. Kaye, Queen Hampton, and Sharon Schmitt. Co-published simultaneously in the *Journal of Library Administration*, (The Haworth Press, Inc.) Vol. 18, No. 1/2, 1993, pp. 15-28; and: *Integrating Total Quality Management in a Library Setting* (ed: Susan Jurow, and Susan B. Barnard) The Haworth Press, Inc., 1993, pp. 15-28. Multiple copies of this article/chapter may be purchased from The Haworth Document Delivery Center. Call 1-800-3-HA-WORTH (1-800-342-9678) between 9:00 - 5:00 (EST) and ask for DOCUMENT DELIVERY CENTER.

tional structures radically different from those that have functioned successfully for years? What would compel any director's review of new management methodologies?

To explore new organizational and management options, with the probable long-term result of radical restructuring, one must act upon certain assumptions. There is no reason for a director to conduct any such exploration if she or he doesn't view research libraries as being in the midst of a major paradigm shift. If we believe that, "If it's not broke, don't fix it!" or that the status quo will continue in a consistent pattern, changing only in intensity and demand, there is no valid reason, other than intellectual curiosity, to review organizational infrastructure options with an eye toward major change.

On the other hand, if we believe that the power of digitized materials, coupled with the transforming nature of information technology tools, is resulting in new patterns in how people learn, think, conduct research, communicate, live, and relate to one another, then any director is compelled, by his or her leadership role and charge, to plan for the future of the organization. In doing so, directors will begin to search out the organizational structures and management methodologies that will complement a pervasive new paradigm of research, learning, and scholarly communication. In fact, the authors believe that we are in the midst of a massive paradigm shift.

A NEW PARADIGM: INTEGRATION AND FLEXIBILITY

We have found at Case Western Reserve University Library (CWRU) that two of the most potent concepts in this new paradigm are the themes of integration and flexibility. At every level, across all services, research libraries and their staffs will certainly require greater flexibility in their ability to respond to users, methodologies, and technologies; they will require a greater range of information management skills, a more integrated approach to problem-solving, and more rapid implementations of solutions; and they will need a greater understanding of the processes that form and drive the accessing, structuring, storage, and retrieval of information, and finally, a thorough, more enriched awareness of users' individual information gathering and usage patterns and behaviors.

Research libraries must seek an organizational approach which will enable them to move easily through an environment characterized by shifting patterns and needs. The emerging demands are intensive and dramatic, and cannot readily be met by existing structures and patterns. The evolving needs of research libraries and research librarians are driven by a number of factors which we must consider and understand.

- Computer-based technology (i.e., any intelligent device that requires some kind of processing chip) and the resulting tools will become exponentially more powerful with each iteration, and each new generation of computing power will emerge with increasing rapidity.
- Software development is being driven by new generations of hardware and peripherals. Each more sophisticated generation of software will increase the demand for faster, more powerful hardware on which to run it. The cycle will feed itself.
- Telecommunication and network infrastructures are becoming more ubiquitous, and the methods of transport along these information highways are steadily more straightforward, portending the removal of time and space barriers on a global basis.
- As software becomes more powerful, more sophisticated, and more accessible, via hardware that is capable of delivering graphics, sound, animation, and full motion video, across networks able to transmit them in real-time, we have certainly entered a generation when some advanced types of personal electronic devices will be available to act as "personal information assistants." These personal electronic devices will be highly cognizant of their owners' individual preferences, needs, and usage patterns. Can librarians and libraries afford to be less so?

While affordable personalized information services offered by small, portable devices are still some way from the retail market, the requirements for powerful, flexible, information management services driven by user needs are here now. In fact, they have always been here, but the limitations of tools and materials have presented very practical barriers to individualized levels of service. But, we can now see that "cookie cutter" services, offered equally to all users in all disciplines, will not continue to meet users' requirements in an era of sophisticated technological tools, where ownership is complemented by access, and a new need emerges for managing the information and knowledge that comes from both.

Librarians are rich in their tradition of service. The services which librarians have historically provided have evolved from a tradition of trying to present the most effective library programs, for the largest number of library users, within the limitations of the available tools, while considering the nature of library materials. Technologically-based tools now possess raw capabilities hitherto unknown. In addition, the materials those tools can access are sparking an evolution in educational approaches.

Library materials can now consist, among others, of photos, speeches, animation, books, magazines, journals, audio cassettes, video cassettes, laser disks, class notes, homework solutions, renderings, readings, and so forth. But, for the first time in civilization's history, all the recorded formats–sight, sound, motion, and text–can be conveyed in one common format: digitization. In their digitized form, all these library materials can be transported wherever networking infrastructures exist, and anyone with the equipment to reach the network can reach the resources it offers.

This paints a vision of access and communication which is sweeping and awesome in its potential. It also speaks to a need for effective management of that access and for thoughtful, powerful, and flexible structuring of that information that will, literally, create the boundary between the users and utter chaos. Never has the wealth of information resources been more prolific. Thus, never has the need to manage them been more critical. This is the power and challenge presented by library materials and tools which research librarians and research libraries must be prepared to manage.

To go a step further, librarians are equipped with skills that go beyond providing powerful informational technologies to facilitate intellectual technologies. Librarians understand the question of validity and reliability of sources, the relevance of materials and citations, the evolution of hypotheses based on existing materials, the weight of terms and descriptors, and the indexing and abstracting of materials that will reveal relationships between them when queried by a search engine.

Librarians understand the nature of research and the process by which information is gathered to produce understanding, and eventually, new knowledge. While this process has occurred throughout history, the capabilities of information technology powerfully support the activities that characterize the synthesis of knowledge: comparing, contrasting, modeling, and querying. Thus, librarians have the ability to design systems that can go beyond information management to knowledge management.[1] Knowledge Management Systems are beginning to facilitate the synthesis of knowledge in new, powerful ways.

The models of service that must evolve to manage knowledge will be driven by the users' needs, in a time-honored library tradition of providing the best possible service to the largest number of users. But, these new and enhanced models of service will certainly not be the same as past models. They cannot be, since the tools, the materials, the users, their world, and the possibilities have all been irrevocably altered. The staffs of research libraries will, of necessity, evolve and execute these new models of service. Thus, the organizational structures that support them, and the management methodologies that guide them, must be tangibly altered as well.

Research libraries now require a highly skilled staff capable of dealing with a concept of information access unprecedented in recorded history. Research library staffs must begin to design information structuring schemes and to prototype information management systems, as opposed to utilizing and consuming the designs of others. Research library staffs are now faced with an information environment characterized by integration rather than discreteness and therefore, staff cannot continue to function in organizational schemes and management methodologies that evolved under very different circumstances in response to a totally different information environment.

As a group of people in an organization structure, library staff have been plagued with difficulties in integrating overlapping functions, as well as in responding with flexibility to changing faculty and student needs. Staff in hierarchical structures are organized best to process packages in discrete functional units. For example, library evaluation mechanisms have tended to focus on production rather than design. Budget constraints have lead to standardization in the creation of access points (AACR II, LC Subject Headings, LC Classification Schedules, etc.). And, quality has often been measured by units processed. But, the information and intellectual technologies which threaten to drown us offer, at the same time, new options for the design and implementation of services, programs, and tools.

We now need a series of organization approaches which draw upon the initiative, creativity, and intellectual abilities both of the individual and the group–for power and momentum require both. And for the first time in decades, we can begin to focus on and be responsive to the unique information environments of faculty and students, as well as their patterns of information gathering and use behaviors.

TQM: A PREFERRED APPROACH FOR A PARADIGM SHIFT

Total Quality Management offers an approach for an organization to design processes, policies, and jobs so that they are the best, most effective methods for serving users' needs, eliminating inefficiencies, and making sure that quality service is built into the way things are done. TQM enables us to focus on performance in order to ensure that people and organizational units possess the competence to follow established processes and procedures consistently and reliably. TQM is an organizational approach which empowers each individual staff member, thoughtfully and appropriately, to contribute to the transformation of the library as an information system.

When directors question the merits of TQM as an appropriate management system for research libraries many questions come readily to mind. For example, should libraries apply Deming's Fourteen Points, Juran's Trilogy of Quality, or Crosby's Four Principles of Quality? What type of organizational structure best supports the TQM management principles? Should staff on all levels become involved immediately in the TQM activities? These are all valid questions that will surface as libraries consider TQM now and in the future, but these are not necessarily the questions that directors should address before deciding to implement TQM.

The value of TQM to the research library is best assessed by considering how it enables library staff to be sensitive to the elements which are key to the creation of the library of the future and to an emerging electronic learning environment. There are three key elements in TQM whether using the Deming, Juran, Crosby, or other approach. These elements enable a library continually to improve processes and performance in order to meet user needs while conforming to standards:

- Knowledge about user needs and commitment to meeting those needs, and ultimately, to exceeding user expectations;
- Leadership that can create a vision based on the needs of users;
- Confidence in staff, that they can deliver quality service to users.

TQM is an important strategic management tool. However, there appears to be some misunderstanding about what quality means. Many organizations, especially nonprofit organizations like libraries, are unsure about the use of "quality" as a management tool because quality as a concept can mean so many things to so many people. With TQM as a context, quality for libraries is defined by library users. Since users' needs will continue to change, quality service will require a continuous improvement process. We will be continually challenged to:

- identify customers—who matters?
- identify customer expectations—what do they want?
- translate expectations into operational processes—what do we need to do to meet user expectations?
- decide on how to measure services—how will we know how we are doing?
- conduct evaluation of services based on established performance measures—what processes should we continue or change?

CWRU's VALUE-ADDED APPROACH

A recent planning project experience at CWRU Library exemplifies a conceptual philosophy of TQM which has the potential to select some of the quality principles from each of the TQM gurus. We did not begin the planning process for the new Kelvin Smith Library[2] at CWRU and the library services it will house with the goal of implementing a TQM approach. Rather, in seeking an analytical structure which could guide our thinking and planning, we selected the model of information systems described by Robert S. Taylor in *Value-Added Process in Information Systems* (Norwood, New Jersey: Ablex, 1986). We found as we proceeded that Taylor's method of value-added analyses has most, if not all, of the essential elements of a TQM approach. Analyzing our CWRU experience with Taylor's model illustrates some of the basic advantages of TQM which became apparent as we proceeded.

In the context of this model, a library will identify both a body of information (the input) and a user group which has a need related to the body of information. The library will provide a service (a value-added process) which somehow enhances this information in relation to the user. The final product is the delivery of this enhanced information to the user. The major focus of Taylor's approach is on defining the usefulness, utility and value of any system solely in terms of what the user considers to be valuable.

At CWRU Library, department heads began to use Taylor's model as a means of describing present services. There are two reasons to describe services in this way. First, once a service has been broken down into value-added components, the service is ready for evaluation by considering other potential value-added processes which might achieve the same or better results. Second, the model is useful in comparing different types of services in order to give a broad description of the library as an information system. The end result of this descriptive process was a set of service paradigms, or functional specifications, that described present services in "value-added" terms.

In order to compare the results of the work by the department heads, and to confirm and expand upon the knowledge that collection managers and reference librarians have about their users, the library conducted an extensive user survey.[3] The librarians conducted interviews and surveys to probe into the information gathering and usage behaviors of the campus community. These focused on what the users' information needs and sources were, how they used this information, and how the library fits into their information environment.

The methodology was an open-ended questionnaire that provided a platform for users to talk freely about information needs. The more than 1400 interviews enabled librarians and users to begin a dialogue around specific questions, resulting in a merging of their respective environments and shared analysis upon which successful planning could be based.

In conjunction with the work of the department heads and the librarians' User Survey, a third group, the Pathways Committee[4] explored the new tools, new formats, and new patterns of scholarly communication which have implications for the functions and decision-making required to support the Kelvin Smith Library. The research of this committee, which consisted of a cross-section of library staff, indicated that librarians, and their users will undergo some major changes. The patterns that describe how scholars will publish findings and communicate with one another will change as the nature of those communication channels evolves. Intellectual property, its management and construction, will be a vital issue. The education, training, and re-training of librarians and library users is an issue that surfaced over and over again as critical to the success of any undertaking. The changes in management requirements and employee skills will necessitate changes in organizational structure. Technology will be ever-present across all fronts, driving some and accommodating others, but remaining, essentially a set of sophisticated tools requiring sophisticated hands at the helm.

The results of the work of the department heads, the User Survey, and the Pathways Committee served as the conceptual framework for the program statement and the recommended enhanced models of service. The service models of the Kelvin Smith Library will be characterized by increased integration of the library's personnel and fiscal resources.

The first type of integration which will continue, is the fusing of the physical library, the electronic learning environment, and the maximum utilization of machine technology to free more staff and user time for higher level information activities, such as analysis of information or interface design.

The second type of integration which will occur will involve the management of the many types of collections available to the CWRU community–on site and remotely housed print and non-print collections and various remotely-accessed digital sources. Toward a seamless integration of these, the resources of collection management and access services will begin to merge, and the tools by which the collections are accessed will move toward a more unified and sophisticated front-end.

The third type of integration which must occur will involve the reorganization of the library. The traditional rigid departmental boundaries of the library will give way to a more flexible form of resource management in which various types of expertise can be brought to bear on problems in a rapid and flexible manner. Task-orientation will be replaced with problem solving.

MANAGING OUR
MOST VALUABLE RESOURCE–
OURSELVES

If one were to place our planning process in the context of TQM, clearly we applied most of Deming's fourteen points and some of Juran's and Crosby's principles as well. Although, our goal was not to implement a TQM project, the results may have been the same because our premise was based on a need to design the most effective processes, policies and jobs to serve user needs while focusing on performance.

We can apply TQM principles to most library operations without embarking on a full-scale TQM project since the guiding TQM principles are sound management tools. But, our CWRU experience indicates that the various TQM models should not be reserved for special projects; they should be considered as an acceptable way of doing business in libraries, now and in the future.

When one contemplates how TQM might work in a research library, the possibilities are limitless, considering the explosive information environment and the changing information needs of library users. "What we are seeing is not isolated change, but changes in almost every environment–changes in how we view humankind, changes in our view of management, changes affecting our knowledge, skills, attitudes, and values. It has been my view for a long time that, before we can begin to talk about change and how people and organizations change, it is essential to have clearly in your mind and heart how you view people."[5]

There is no doubt from the CWRU experience that TQM principles can work in libraries, but one must know how to work within the TQM concepts. TQM works best as we manage our most valuable resource–ourselves. The library of the future can only be created by the librarian of the future. The most important element of a successful TQM program is its inherent philosophy of managing people. Second, TQM requires that research library staff define progress in terms of meeting users' needs. Thus, the research library application of TQM has library staff functioning as valued partners in the process of meeting customer or library user needs. Directors must lead in the creation of a management culture that encourages employees to contribute and gives staff the necessary training in an organized way.

To provide quality services to users, it is also essential that directors develop and communicate to staff on all levels a clear vision of the library's future. It must be a vision that states: here is what we are, here is what we do, here is where we are heading, and here is what is important and unique about our library. Directors must have confidence in their staff that they can deliver quality service to library users and the commitment to act on recommended changes.

TRANSFORMING THE RESEARCH LIBRARY

The transforming nature of information technologies, intellectual technologies, and digitization is awesome in its potential, and challenging in its scope. TQM provides a context, a philosophy, and a structure for enabling library staff to, in turn, transform the research library into a responsive and flexible information system.

Deming observed that there are two kinds of problems–those of today and those of tomorrow. He accurately stated that it "is easy to stay bound up in the tangled knot of problems of today, becoming ever more and more efficient in them."[6] Directors must provide a vision framed around the problems of tomorrow and organizational structures that will enable staff to implement continually evolving models of service to solve those problems.

NOTES

1. Traditionally academic libraries have acted to identify, access, and deliver the materials they housed in support of their institution's curriculum, faculty, students, and staff. Ownership was virtually the only guarantee of access and the library acted partially as a warehouser of containers of knowledge. Printed indexes, abstracts, bibliographies, study guides, etc., all provided access to those various containers. With the advent of electronic technologies a new tool for managing information resources emerged, a tool with "transforming" potential. Electronic technologies not only can perform many of the labor intensive tasks associated with accessing and tracking "containers of knowledge," they are capable of breaking down the barriers of containers and permitting an intellectual access not possible with other kinds of technologies.

It is now possible to digitize all kinds of information including images, photographs, sounds, text, and animation. Computers can store anything that can be digitized. This digitized data can be structured to allow for very focused, detailed searching. Librarians can design control mechanisms to allow scholars to retrieve a wide range of materials directly applicable to their research and teaching. These control mechanisms do not force the scholar to utilize the information in whatever form it originally appears in the "container," but allows the scholar to derive individual views of the data that directly pertain to the scholar's work. The system that brings together the hardware, software, control mechanisms, online resources, and human expertise and makes them available to scholars is known as Knowledge Management (KM).

Knowledge Management is a means by which librarians can help scholars and universities retain control of the intellectually generated property that is their most precious and valuable commodity. It is a way of structuring new works as they are created, so that they are maximally accessible and a way of accessing existing resources to enable the highest level of integration with the scholar's work, helping to create new knowledge. Knowledge Management environments consist of:

- complex, high quality, dynamic databases that are critical to daily work;
- integrated electronic systems and services;
- online tools to collaboratively build, maintain, share, and use databases;
- interface tools for access to multiple local and remote databases.

Some of the examples of types of online tools available for use in KM systems include:

- editing tools
- graphics tools
- database management tools
- analysis tools
- peer review tools

Successful Knowledge Management environments require that the databases constructed consist of data that is critical to the given scholarly community and that the scholarly community form vital alliances with the librarians.

A critical feature of any Knowledge Management system is that it is constructed by a collaborative effort between librarians and the scholar, so that the control mechanisms involved produce highly relevant search results that match the scholars' information gathering and usage patterns.

Excerpted from: "Kelvin Smith Library. The Electronic Learning Environment: Transforming Access to Knowledge. A Program Statement" (Cleveland, OH: Case Western Reserve University, 1992), 159-160.

2. The Kelvin Smith Library is the new twenty-seven million dollar library facility to be constructed on the campus of Case Western Reserve University. When Case Western Reserve University made a decision to centralize its largest library sites and to construct a new library, it did so with the notion that it would not be constructing a classical library or any library that had previously existed, but a new kind of library, a library designed to complement CWRU's Electronic Learning Environment, a library that would not only function and flourish in the future, but would point the way for the rest of the campus scholarly community.

Excerpted from: Sharon Schmitt, "Summary of Background Work for the Kelvin Smith Library" (Cleveland, OH: Case Western Reserve University, 1992), 5.

3. The User Survey Committee, appointed by the Director of University Library in November of 1991, was asked to explore how faculty, students, and staff gather information to determine what impact different information seeking behaviors might have upon services and programs as we plan for the Kelvin Smith Library. More specifically, the Committee's charge was to (1) confirm and expand upon the knowledge that librarians have about library users', and potential users', information environments: what the users information needs and sources are, and how University Library fits into that information environment, and (2) the participation of the librarians will further strengthen their relationships and responsibilities with faculty and students in building the University Library collections and services.

To prepare for the survey a series of planning and training documents were created and reviewed to familiarize committee members with methods of data collection and analysis, tips on how to design a questionnaire, and interviewing techniques. The committee began its work with brainstorming sessions to conceptualize the project, to develop a questionnaire, and to establish goals. After much deliberation, it was decided to design a questionnaire with open ended questions to probe into the information gathering patterns and behaviors of the campus community and to track current services. Equal emphasis was placed on the process as well as the content of the project.

The methodology was an open ended questionnaire that was administered by the librarians. These information specialists conducted one-on-one and group interviews, concentrating on the primary constituents of University Library–faculty and students, and staff of the Colleges and Weatherhead School of Management (WSOM). The one-on-one and group interviewing approach provided an arena for relationship building and collaborative information sharing. It was more challenging to interview a few individuals who required more structured questions and responses. The average interview took 30-45 minutes. The interviews enabled both parties (librarian and/or faculty, student, and staff) to begin a dialogue around specific questions, resulting in a merging of their respective environments and a shared analysis upon which successful planning could be based.

The committee interviewed and surveyed 1403 individuals from the CWRU community. That number represents 274 faculty members (70% of the full and part time professors), 525 graduate students (16% of the full and part time professional students from the Colleges and WSOM), 491 undergraduate students (18% of the full time and part time students from the Colleges including the School of Nursing), and 112 administrators and staff members. The more than 1400 interviews are representative of more than 100 campus departments, including vice presidents, deans, trustees, department chairs, and directors of departments.

Excerpted from: Queen Hampton, "The Final Report of the User Survey Committee" (Cleveland, OH: Case Western Reserve University, 1992), 1-3.

4. The Pathways Committee consisted of ten staff members, both professional and support staff, from all areas of the library.

5. D. Kaye Gapen, "Transition and Change: Technical Services at the Center." LRTS 33 (1987):287.

6. Terry Mackey and Kitty Mackey, "Think Quality! The Deming Approach Does Work in Libraries." *Library Journal* (May 1992):58.

Organizational Development and TQM: The Harvard College Library's Experience

Mary Elizabeth Clack

INTRODUCTION

In the Harvard College Library, the decision to explore the concept and techniques of total quality management (TQM) evolved as a result of, and in conjunction with, the Library's strategic planning initiative. Our study of the principles of TQM, its applicability in a university library setting, and our experience with various aspects of quality training comprise an ongoing effort. Total quality initiatives at Harvard are based on the needs of each unit or department. Consulting and training support are available through the Harvard Quality Process, an adaptation of TQM training developed at Harvard in cooperation with the Xerox Corporation. The Harvard Quality Process began offering problem-solving training in the University's Office for Information Technology. Other groups of staff from, for example, the Office of the Vice President for Administration,

Mary Elizabeth Clack is Staff Development Officer and Serial Records Librarian at Harvard College Library, Cambridge, MA.

[Haworth co-indexing entry note]: "Organizational Development and TQM: The Harvard College Library's Experience." Clack, Mary Elizabeth. Co-published simultaneously in the *Journal of Library Administration*, (The Haworth Press, Inc.) Vol. 18, No. 1/2, 1993, pp. 29-43; and: *Integrating Total Quality Management in a Library Setting* (ed: Susan Jurow, and Susan B. Barnard), The Haworth Press, Inc., 1993, pp. 29-43. Multiple copies of this article/chapter may be purchased from The Haworth Document Delivery Center. Call 1-800-3-HAWORTH (1-800-342-9678) between 9:00 - 5:00 (EST) and ask for DOCUMENT DELIVERY CENTER.

the Facilities Maintenance Department, and the Kennedy School of Government have been trained. In the Library, elements of TQM have been found to be particularly germane to organizational development goals and the future of the organization. This article will summarize the brief history of the Library's experience with TQM and its plans for a pilot implementation and training process.

THE IMPETUS: THE FORCES OF CHANGE

The impetus for an organizational development process in the Harvard College Library arose from the groundwork laid by the Strategic Planning Retreat Group. In the fall of 1990, the Library embarked on a strategic planning process under the leadership of Richard De Gennaro, Roy E. Larsen Librarian of Harvard College. An important aspect of this process was the attention given to the role of staff and organizational development in shaping a vision for the Library's future. The last portion of the Vision Statement crafted by the Strategic Planning Retreat Group highlights the changing nature of staff roles and responsibilities in an era of pervasive change:

> There will be increasing experimentation and innovation within the Library, particularly with regard to scholarly communication. More members of the Library's staff will carry multiple responsibilities that cut across lines separating traditional functions. Both technological competence and solid traditional skills will be required. The Library's growing dynamism and broadening concerns will require a major investment in staff development. (The text of the entire Vision Statement appears in Appendix A.)

THE TASK FORCE ON STAFF AND ORGANIZATIONAL DEVELOPMENT

The next step in the process was the formation of five task forces, one of which was devoted to staff and organizational development.[1] The charge to the HCL Strategic Planning Committee's Task Force on Staff and Organizational Development focused on designing elements of an organizational development strategy in a changing library environment. It stated:

> Positive adaptation to change must become the hallmark of the Harvard College Library over the next ten years. Whether this will be so or not will depend in large part on the kind of organization we develop.

It is important to note the emphasis on organizational development, a deliberate process of planned change which incorporates a "long-range effort to improve an organization's problem-solving and renewal processes, particularly through a more effective and collaborative management of organizational culture."[2]

The Task Force's objective was to formulate recommendations for an organizational development strategy after assessing the status quo and envisioning a new organizational culture. In this mature organization, characterized by a good degree of stability in the past, attention was turning to ways to renew and revitalize the organizational culture. Early on it was recognized that such a process should necessarily develop increased flexibility in all staff to respond to unplanned change, as well as actively plan for change, with all staff becoming more effective in improving processes and service.

THE TASK FORCE:
COMPOSITION AND RECOMMENDATIONS

In January 1991, the Task Force on Staff and Organizational Development began five months of weekly meetings leading to the preparation of its final report. Its membership, like that of the other task forces, included staff at all levels and representatives from many of the eleven units which comprise the Harvard College Library.[3] For staff and organizational development, this was particularly important, since much of the richness of the Library resides in the diversity of its staff. Moreover, a critical factor in planning, especially for organizational development, is the ability to benefit from multiple perspectives. The Task Force gradually grew into a team that reached decisions by consensus, collaborated closely on projects, and respected individual differences. This broadly-based team approach is a distinguishing characteristic of the ongoing initiative.

It would be impossible to summarize adequately the contents of the Task Force's interim and final reports here, because the recommendations covered several priority areas for change. But the findings which led the Task Force to recommend more in-depth study of quality management principles and techniques in the design of an organizational development process can be presented.

PRIORITY AREAS FOR CHANGE

The Task Force's attention turned first to an examination of the norms, espoused values, and underlying assumptions that constituted the Library's organizational culture. We identified many positive elements. Among them were pride in individual accomplishments, an appreciation of diversity, the advantages of decentralization, strong peer communication, clear communication channels, and the value placed on high standards, detailed documentation, and the use of technology.

At the same time, an informal survey was conducted by the Task Force. This survey was an abbreviated version of a questionnaire designed by Rensis Likert, covering six dimensions: leadership, motivation, communication, decision-making, goals and control. The results, confirmed by information from staff focus groups, brought to light some priority areas for improvement or change. Staff expressed an interest in more involvement in decision-making and goal-setting. They wished to have a better sense of the "big picture," including how their jobs contribute to the accomplishment of library goals. They thought that greater trust and open communication in all directions were needed throughout the Library. People also raised concerns about adaptation to change and the integration of new tasks, responsibilities, and projects with existing job demands.

ARRIVING AT A NEW CULTURE

Taking the above results into consideration, the Task Force delineated the shifts necessary to arrive at the new organizational culture depicted in the Vision Statement. Among the more important shifts were:

- From decentralization to a shared vision of unity amidst diversity,
- From specialization and segmentation of tasks to an integrated view of tasks,
- From an emphasis on individual accomplishments to a recognition of the efficacy of collaboration,
- From a reactive environment with sporadic change to a dynamic environment characterized by innovation and risk-taking,
- From a rigid process culture to one with flexible responses to different situations,
- From a hierarchically governed organization toward one with trust in, and participation of, staff at all levels.

We advocated the creation of a new culture that would emphasize unity, integration, collaboration, and trust and invest in training so that all staff may develop as individuals and as team members. Implicit in such a developmental strategy would be respect for the talents, experiences, and opinions of staff at all levels.

CONSIDERING TQM

About the time we were completing this informal diagnosis, we discussed our findings with two key resource persons assigned to the Task Force: Constance Towler, Director of the Harvard Quality Process, and Douglas Renick, Consultant at the Center for Training and Development. Both were actively training groups of staff in other university departments in the Harvard Quality Process, an adaptation of TQM training developed in cooperation with the Xerox Corporation. They introduced us to the concepts of TQM, and we began actively researching TQM. It became readily apparent that many elements of TQM addressed areas for change we had identified as priority areas.

Some of these elements are:

1. Service excellence–A desire to maintain or strengthen the commitment to the Library's philosophy of service to users.
2. Employee involvement and team building–The importance of group process skills in fostering collaboration, trust, open and honest communication, and a more structured and consistent approach to teamwork and problem-solving.
3. An investment in ongoing training and skill building–The Library will be seen as a "learning organization" in its efforts to stay abreast of changes in its internal and external environment and to increase its capacity for revitalization and renewal.
4. Process/systems focus–Providing a way to gain more knowledge of whole processes and to keep them open to critical analysis and evaluation.
5. Continuous improvement–Rethinking workflows and streamlining processes to achieve new goals.
6. Cooperation across boundaries–With the growing complexity of problems and opportunities facing the Library, collaboration across traditional departmental boundaries is critical.

The Task Force was careful to acknowledge that in some libraries and departments, teamwork, service excellence, and cooperation across boundaries were already salient features of the environment, independent of a quality process. From the outset, the goal of the organizational development effort has been the encouragement of a more consistent and universal application of teamwork, cooperation across boundaries, and collaboration, supported by a coordinated training effort.

The Task Force completed in its final report and held an open meeting to air its recommendations in June 1991. The effort had been launched.

THE STEERING COMMITTEE: ONGOING SUPPORT FOR ORGANIZATIONAL DEVELOPMENT

Work on organizational development resumed in the fall of 1991. The Librarian of Harvard College appointed me half-time as Staff

Development Officer and the Steering Committee on Staff and Organizational Development was formed. This group was entrusted with the ongoing support of staff and organizational development and charged with examining aspects of TQM that would be applied to the process.

Since October 1991, the Steering Committee, comprised of some former Task Force members and other volunteers, has held some forty meetings. Its nine members (seven professionals and two support staff) represent all levels of staff and several library units (Widener, Cabot, Houghton, Tozzer, Lamont/Hilles and HCL Personnel). Its sponsor is Susan Lee, Associate Librarian for Administrative Services.[4]

In the course of its work, the Steering Committee developed the two figures which accompany this article. Figure 1 outlines the key elements of a staff and organizational development process using a quality tool, the fishbone diagram. Figure 2 is a model illustrating the integrated parts of the process with Strategic Planning at the core.

THE STEERING COMMITTEE

The Steering Committee guides the effort. Its agenda includes:

- ongoing research on the principles and applications of TQM in the academic library environment, providing reading materials to interested staff, and exchanging materials with other interested libraries.
- benchmarking–Study of the TQM efforts of other organizations in order to discover relevant applications for libraries. In addition to other libraries and universities, some of the Library's vendors have quality initiatives in place.
- training–As a group, Committee members attended six half-days of the Harvard Quality Process Problem-Solving Training. This module included effective meeting skills, interactive and consensus-building skills, and problem-solving skills using the six-step model developed by the Xerox Corporation. A case study was used to facilitate understanding and application of the steps in the process.
- communication–A broad-based communication program including:

1. A publication in newsletter format entitled "HCL Cornerstone" serves as a vehicle for updating staff on Steering Committee activities and summarizing its meetings with different groups of staff.
2. Open meetings for all staff–The first meetings were held in March 1992; the agenda included a summary of Steering Committee activities, brief presentations by each Committee member on training in effective meeting skills and interactive skills, followed by questions and discussion.
3. Meeting with the two College Library Joint Councils–In April 1992, the Steering Committee met with the Joint Councils, the groups of representatives of management and the Harvard Union of Clerical and Technical Workers who meet to discuss and investigate workplace issues and prepare policies for management's implementation. We discussed our common interests, the background of the Committee, and described elements of TQM and our training experiences. A lively discussion followed, and the two groups agreed to work together to reach the common goal of improving the quality of worklife in the HCL.
4. Meeting with HCL Heads and Managers–In May 1992, the Committee met with the Library's managers to present its activities as depicted in the accompanying Figures 1 and 2.

LEADERSHIP

Managers play a key role in supporting the process through ongoing communication and training. They sense the urgency and value of the effort and encourage "cognitive redefinition"[5] enroute to the new organizational culture. Managers can set the stage for strategic thinking and team formation, act as role models for facilitative leadership, and utilize their professional contacts for benchmarking library processes and policies.

COMMUNICATION

The glue of an organizational development process is communication. Staff are responsible for creating and utilizing formal and infor-

FIGURE 1. SUPPORTING ELEMENTS OF AN ORGANIZATIONAL DEVELOPMENT PROCESS

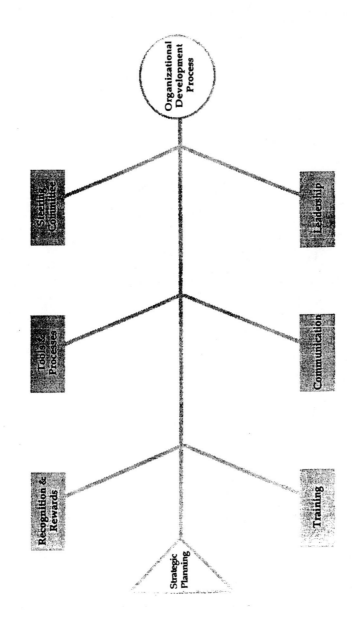

FIGURE 2. A QUALITY-INSPIRED MODEL FOR ORGANIZATIONAL DEVELOPMENT IN THE HARVARD COLLEGE LIBRARY (Adapted from the GOAL/QPC TQM WHEEL by the Steering Committee)

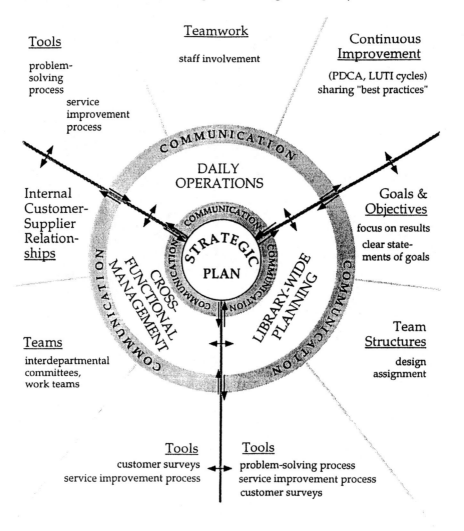

Tools

problem-
solving
process
 service
 improvement
 process

Teamwork

staff involvement

Continuous
Improvement

(PDCA, LUTI cycles)
sharing "best practices"

Internal
Customer-
Supplier
Relation-
ships

COMMUNICATION

DAILY
OPERATIONS

COMMUNICATION

STRATEGIC
PLAN

CROSS-
FUNCTIONAL
MANAGEMENT

LIBRARY-WIDE
PLANNING

Goals &
Objectives

focus on results

clear state-
ments of goals

Teams

interdepartmental
committees,
work teams

Team
Structures

design
assignment

Tools

customer surveys
service improvement process

Tools

problem-solving process
service improvement process
customer surveys

mal communication networks. Appropriate timing and comprehensiveness of communiqués explaining strategic objectives are important organizational values.

TRAINING

The library should become a "learning organization" which values team building and functional training. In the long term, training would have a cascading effect, consisting of a "train the trainers" process to ensure continuity and availability of in-house resource persons.

TOOLS AND PROCESSES

Relevant quality tools and processes will be introduced and utilized in the quality training process. Examples are flowcharts, cause-and-effect (fishbone) diagrams, GANTT charts, and PERT charts. It will be important for teams to share "best practices" as processes are refined and improved.

RECOGNITION AND REWARDS

Our goal is to broaden our performance appraisal system to recognize both individual achievement and collaborative skills. Definition of recognition and rewards requires wider discussion and participation by staff members at all levels.

The model represented in Figure 2 was adapted from the GOAL/QPC TQM wheel™ by the Steering Committee. The core is the strategic plan, defined operationally throughout the Library. Communication pervades the model, integrating the concepts. The model incorporates major themes in each area: setting goals and objectives through library-wide planning, employing continuous improvement in daily operations, and analyzing various internal and external "customer" relationships by cross-functional/cross-departmental teams. The major functions in each area are supported by team structures and the tools of quality management, most notably problem-solving tools and techniques and service improvement processes.

FUTURE PLANS

The Steering Committee spent the summer of 1992 working on several projects which will come to fruition in the fall. These include:

- Preparation of a brochure that outlines the goals of the training sessions, the training modules and methodology and introduces the trainers.
- Developing a workshop on organizational change for Library staff in which participants will examine the change process, assess their readiness for change, and develop a personal plan for change.
- Collaborating with trainers in the Harvard Quality Process on the design of the Group Process and problem-solving training, including writing a library-specific case study.
- Serving as resource persons for members of the Cataloging Services Department who will be the first group of staff to attend training sessions. This department is being reorganized into a team structure and its space is being reconfigured. Staff members will be examining and rethinking work processes; thus the Department was considered an appropriate environment in which to receive training in tools and process management.

In addition, library managers will attend a two-day workshop including updates on facets of the Strategic Plan. Included will be an introduction to TQM in libraries presented by the Association of Research Libraries' Office of Management Services.

CONCLUSION

The Task Force on Staff and Organizational Development proposed a developmental human resources strategy, comprehensive in scope and including all staff. In a process of organizational development and planned change, the principles of TQM, including participation in planning and examining and improving work processes, are useful and relevant. TQM also reinforces the service objectives critical to the Library's success. The strengths of the Harvard College Library's approach lie in the broadly-based membership of the Steering Committee, the members' commitment to group process, and the ongoing communication efforts that keep it attuned to staff needs.

The support of the Library's leadership who encourage staff to reconsider roles, responsibilities, policies and practices, is critical. If this ongoing process of personal and organizational renewal continues to be supported, we will reshape our organizational culture, drawing on past traditions and new tools to strengthen future initiatives. The training process will be one of the factors which will lead the Library to develop a collective sense of identity and purpose and staff commitment to fulfilling the Library's mission in times of uncertainty and change.

NOTES

1. The other task forces were on Collections, Intellectual Access, Services and Space.

2. James M. Higgins. *Human Resources: Concepts and Skills.* (New York: Random House, 1982), p. 333.

3. The Harvard College Library consists of the central collections of the Faculty of Arts and Sciences (7.3 million volumes) with a staff of 448 including 168 librarians and 280 support staff. In addition to Widener (social sciences and humanities) the libraries include Cabot Science, Fine Arts, Harvard Yenching (East Asia), Houghton (rare books), Kummel (geology), Lamont and Hilles (undergraduate), Littauer (economics), Music, and Tozzer (anthropology).

4. A "sponsor" is usually a high level manager to whom the team reports; the sponsor is not a team member, but approves the results of, and signs off on, each action step taken by the team. (From Barnard, Susan B. "A Draft Model for Adapting TQM in a Research Library." Washington, D.C.: Association of Research Libraries Office of Management Services, January 25, 1992.)

5. According to Schein, "cognitive redefinition" results in developing new assumptions, which are at the core of organizational culture. Cognitive redefinition occurs through "teaching, coaching, changing the structure and processes when necessary, consistently paying attention to and rewarding evidence of learning the new ways . . . " (Schein, Edgar. *Organizational Culture and Leadership.* San Francisco: Jossey-Bass, 1989, p. 295.)

APPENDIX A

THE HARVARD COLLEGE LIBRARY, TEN YEARS HENCE

The Harvard College Library, as one of the world's preeminent research libraries, will remain nationally and internationally prominent for the depth and breadth of its collections. The library will continue to acquire, organize, house, preserve, and make available materials that support teaching and research in the Faculty of Arts and Sciences. Library collections will include traditional manuscript, printed and artifactual materials as well as audio-visual and electronic resources.

As academic fields continue to develop diverse patterns of research and communication, the College Library will respond with a growing array of specialized resources and services. Such a response will take place within the framework of Harvard's traditional pattern of decentralized services closely allied to the needs of particular University constituencies. Increasing reliance on shared automation systems will bolster the administrative coordination necessary to manage decentralization.

An expanded online system will provide access to both library holdings and other scholarly and information resources on campus. All card catalogs will have been eliminated through comprehensive retrospective conversion. While continuing to build and describe its own collections, the library will also provide access to external information resources. To an increasing extent it will participate in cooperative activities, including resource sharing, as a means to this enhanced access. Cooperation will also enable the library to operate more efficiently and to contribute to the worldwide community of scholars.

The College Library will pursue a deliberate strategy of identifying and satisfying user needs. Information services will be tailored to meet differing instructional and research needs. Programs to train users in locating, using, and managing information will complement more traditional reference services.

The use of facilities will be integrated to meet the changing needs of users, staff, and collections. A growing proportion of the College Library's holdings will be housed off-site. An ongoing program will ensure that materials receiving regular use or requiring immediate access are housed on campus, while other materials will be held off campus. Improved facilities will be available on campus for servicing audio-visual resources, electronic information, manuscript and other non-published materials, microforms, government documents, and other types of research materials requiring specialized equipment or services.

There will be increasing experimentation and innovation within the

Library, particularly with regard to scholarly communication. More members of the Library's staff will carry multiple responsibilities that cut across the lines separating traditional functions. Both technological competence and solid traditional skills will be required. There will be an emphasis on collaboration and developing shared understandings and shared strategies. The College Library's growing dynamism, broadening concerns, and new initiatives will require a major investment in ongoing training and staff development at all levels.

The Vision Statement is Appendix B of "Commitment to Renewal: a Strategic Plan for the Harvard College Library," Feb. 3, 1992, p. 20.

Total Quality Management:
The Oregon State University Library's Experience

Karyle S. Butcher

BACKGROUND

In Winter 1990, the staff and faculty at the Libraries of Oregon State University were offered an opportunity to hear a presentation on the work the University was doing with Total Quality Management (TQM). Total Quality Management had been introduced to the OSU campus in 1989, but most of the library staff had no real understanding of what it was and how it could be applied to a library organization. The University Vice President for Finance and Administration described a process which would allow for "organization-wide participation in planning and implementing a continuous improvement process."[1] The University had a variety of reasons for promoting TQM. Increasing demands for service and rising costs resulting from inflation were becoming the standard for Oregon, all combined with drastically decreasing revenue.

Karyle S. Butcher is Assistant University Librarian for Research and Public Services at Oregon State University, Corvallis, OR.

[Haworth co-indexing entry note]: "Total Quality Management: The Oregon State University Library's Experience." Butcher, Karyle S. Co-published simultaneously in the *Journal of Library Administration,* (The Haworth Press, Inc.) Vol. 18, No. 1/2, 1993, pp. 45-56; and: *Integrating Total Quality Management in a Library Setting* (ed: Susan Jurow, and Susan B. Barnard), The Haworth Press, Inc., 1993, pp. 45-56. Multiple copies of this article/chapter may be purchased from The Haworth Document Delivery Center. Call 1-800-3-HA-WORTH (1-800-342-9678) between 9:00 - 5:00 (EST) and ask for DOCUMENT DELIVERY CENTER.

There was a need to provide the same or increasing services without an increase in personnel or other resources. At the same time, the intent of university officials was to insure that the service being offered was of increasing quality. According to Coate's presentation, TQM had enabled those areas in the University which implemented it to accomplish improved quality service with the same work force. They were able to do this by following a prescribed methodology which included utilizing customer surveys, flowcharting work processes, analyzing the data, brainstorming solutions, developing performance standards, and selecting and implementing solutions. Unlike some other management theories, TQM does not promise a major turnaround in the organization. Its hallmark is its emphasis on the process, not on personnel. W. Edwards Deming, a pioneer of the TQM methodology, repeatedly states that, in most cases, when an organization uses TQM, it will discover that ninety percent of the problems are caused by faulty processes, and only ten percent are related to personnel. Finally, change, according to TQM, comes through small incremental steps rather than overnight transformations. Therefore, organizations implementing quality management must look for long-term solutions and be willing to make the concomitant long-term commitment. TQM is clearly not a quick fix.

LOOKING AT THE TQM PROCESS

Although their reaction to the first presentation was mixed, the Library Administration[2] in conjunction with Library Division Heads agreed to participate in a three-day TQM training program. The intent of the program was to learn more about quality management and to explore the possibilities of using TQM processes in a library environment. The agreement the Director of Libraries established with the group was that each of the twelve members of the group would attempt to put aside any prejudices against TQM, and participate as fully as possible in the three-day program. In return, the Director of Libraries agreed that any decision to embark on quality management in the library would be made by the entire group.

The training session was conducted by two facilitator/trainers who were employed by Oregon State University. The first half of the first day was close to a disaster. The trainers' enthusiasm for TQM was leading them to proselytize rather than train. In addition to providing information about the TQM process, they were also interested in having the library commit to the program. If they were successful, the library would become the first academic unit on campus to participate in TQM. Unfortunately, the intensity of their enthusiasm was disconcerting and during the lunch hour some members of the group were ready to abandon the training. Because of this, the afternoon session began with a forthright discussion on what the group found bothersome about both the presentation and TQM.

Some of the concern was simply with the TQM vocabulary. Words such as "customer" and "quality control" were, according to some participants, fine for business but not for academia. University Vice President Coate, writing on impediments to TQM, discusses what he defines as this barrier of language. "For faculty, the notion of a buyer (the student customer) and a seller (faculty member) transacting a product (knowledge) for a price (tuition) is too crude and dispassionate a description of the education enterprise."[3] Coate continues by noting that arguments about language are time-consuming and, as happened with the library group, never resolved. In spite of more acceptance in libraries of the concept of the active "customer" rather than the passive "patron," a library embarking on investigation of TQM will need to appreciate the potential disturbances the language of quality management can cause. In Oregon's case, the group recognized that the jargon of TQM was offensive to some members, but they agreed that inventing a new jargon was not a worthwhile use of time.

Another area of concern was that TQM was simply the latest megatrend in an ongoing series of organizational theories, and that it really offered the library nothing different from what was currently practiced. Those adhering to this view noted the library had already made use of participating groups for problem solving. The use of committees which included both library faculty and classified staff had been a long-standing tradition in the library. Many in the group also believed that the library was already committed to quality service and that, while TQM might work in some organizations, it offered nothing new to the library. For these people, TQM looked to be another way of reorganizing work which was neither more nor less effective than what was currently being done. Another less-articulated view, but one which was an underlying concern for some, was the fear that TQM was a means of removing middle managers. If TQM made the workers into leaders, what would happen to the middle managers?

In the second and third days of the training an attempt was made to answer these concerns and further examine how TQM might be used in the library. In order to help the group look at TQM from a different perspective, the trainers asked them to describe the services currently provided by the library. They then asked what services would be provided if more money or personnel were made available. As is the case with many librarians, we were strong believers in services and very quickly produced a list of what could be and was being done, and given additional resources, what they could do. The TQM trainers challenged their thinking. They asked: How did the library know it was providing quality services? Who determined what services the library provided? How were such services measured and by whom?

These questions provoked a heated discussion about customer surveys and their usefulness as a means of determining service needs. Some of the group worried that such surveys would result in unrealistic demands and expectations. They feared that most library users had narrow interests, and if asked to articulate what they thought the library should be, would see only the small picture. Thus, a survey of science faculty would likely show that group wanting primarily journals while a survey of undergraduates would result in a demand for more monographs. A few of the group worried that customer surveys had the potential for setting up false expectations. A further concern was that relying on the wants of the customer as a determiner of what the library should contain was in conflict with the professional expertise of the library faculty.

The TQM presenters tried to alleviate these concerns by explaining that the value of the surveys was not to have the customer declare how the library should run, but rather to help the library determine how closely its view of the wants of the users reflected the reality of what the library provided. They noted that the library might be doing something quite well (such as maintaining a card file) but if there is no demand for it, the library is not using its resources wisely. In these times of scarcity, it is poor management of personnel and other resources to continue to do something which is no longer needed. As the group thought about this idea, they realized that the library had not examined basic services based on customer needs. Generally, services were added or eliminated based on availability of personnel, money and in-house assessments.

On the last day of the training, the group went through a TQM exercise determining what the critical processes of the library were. In the Oregon State University model of TQM, critical processes are those processes which the University President and his cabinet determine are essential to the health of the university. These processes are reflected in OSU's vision statement and long-range plan and include, among others: teaching, information service, research and funding development. Using the University's critical processes as a point of reference, the trainers asked the group to list what they viewed as the essential processes of the library. When the group reconvened, the Director of Libraries was asked to be the first to put his critical processes on the board. This was followed by the group posting their critical processes.

One thing which was immediately clear to everyone was the consistency of processes. Although there were items identified by individual members which no one else identified, there was general agreement among the group on major concerns. By the end of the three-day session a list of the library's five critical processes had been developed–Access, Staff Development, Effective Management, User/Patron Orientation, and Technology, as determined by the Director of Libraries. In addition, each person had a list of the processes critical to his or her unit. However, the group had not yet determined if the library would try TQM. That decision would be made when they reconvened at a later date in the library.

UNDERTAKING TQM IN THE LIBRARY

After the initial training, the eight Library Division Heads, along with the four members of Library Administration, met to determine whether or not to make a commitment to using TQM. In addition to the considerations previously mentioned (e.g., greater efficiency, improved service, and better utilization of resources), there was a political consideration. Clearly, TQM had the support of the University President. Just as clearly, other academic units on campus were wary of entering into a process for organizational change which had such echoes of the business world. This was an opportunity for the library to be on the cutting edge of university planning by being the first academic unit to venture into quality management territory. Not only would we gain instant visibility on campus, but we would have the advantage of getting in at the ground floor, while resources were still available for training.

After weighing the time commitment, the possibility that library staff might view TQM as a means for streamlining and perhaps eliminating their jobs, and the potential political advantages, it was agreed to try two pilot teams. Both teams would be in the public services sector of the library. One team would look at the reshelving process in the library while the other would look at the flow of government publications from the time they arrived in the library until they appeared on the shelf available to the public.

WORKING WITH THE TQM MODEL

The initial step in the TQM process is for an administrator, in this case the Assistant University Librarian for Research and Public Services, to agree to be the *sponsor* of a team. The *team leader* is the head of the unit which is being studied. In the case of the library units involved, the supervisor of Stack Maintenance, a paraprofessional position, was the team leader for the Shelving Team, while the Government Publications librarian, a professional position, headed up the Documents Team. Each team also had a *facilitator* who was not an employee of the library and who was selected from a university-wide pool. Since the person selected as facilitator is not from the library, that person is able to keep the team focused on the TQM process and not get involved with the personalities of the team. Moreover, for the library to obtain the services of an outside facilitator, it needed to be willing to provide one to other campus departments. While this method has meant an added time commitment for the library, it has the double advantage of exposing library staff to TQM and providing library presence throughout the university.

The *team* is composed of those people who are owners of the process, i.e., they must do the work. This is different from the way in which the library appointed work groups or committees prior to using TQM. When a committee was appointed to study an issue, common practice was to include all points of view related to the issue. This has resulted in situations where the committee's recommended solution may not take into account those who are responsible for implementation. This, in turn, leads to no solution or partial solution, creating the feeling that, "You put in all of that work and nothing ever happens." TQM methodology mandates not only that the owners be members of the team, but also that once a team is established, the team leader meet regularly with the team sponsor. This process helps to insure that the actions taken by the team are acceptable to the sponsor and, ultimately, to the Library Administration. These very simple steps–having those who do the work be on the team and having regular sign offs on team progress–are two essentials which differentiate a TQM team from other library committees and from the earlier concept of quality circles.

In the case of the library's first two teams, those doing the work also included staff from outside of Stack Maintenance and Government Publications. Although this was a workable approach with the Shelving Team, it complicated the Documents Team, which actually had too many members. Owners of the work included representatives from cataloging, serials, and government publications for a total of eleven participants. Although the team ultimately was successful in terms of implementing its first two recommendations, its size and differing personalities hindered its ability to find a common time to meet and to work together successfully. On the other hand, the six-person Shelving Team included as owners not only those directly responsible for shelving, but also a staff member from the Circulation Unit. This person was able to provide useful information on how returned materials were processed by Circulation, and on the types of questions customers seeking materials from the shelves were asking. Based on this experience, it is preferable for a library starting its first teams to start simply with small teams and avoid crossing over too many departmental lines.

A second difficulty the library encountered with its first two teams was in their surveys. The intent of the preliminary survey is to refine the original charge of each team. This is done by preparing a brief set of questions directed at the library's external customers. Both teams had difficulties in drafting a concise set of questions and in determining how to reach those customers who were not regular library users. Moreover, by the time the teams were ready to do the surveys, summer session had started and identifying groups to contact outside of the library was difficult. Ultimately, the teams had to rely heavily on surveying those individuals who came to the library.

An unforeseen benefit of the survey process derived from the survey of library staff, or internal customers, since staff are also users of the services provided by Documents and Stack Maintenance, the TQM survey provided them an opportunity to express their opinions in a neutral manner. Surveying the staff also gave both teams an opportunity to do some continuing education since both teams discovered that much of the library staff and faculty were unaware of the services the two units were providing. In addition, when they examined the results of their surveys, the teams discovered a number of peripheral issues that were not within the province of the team to address, but which suggested a response by the Library Administration. For example, the Shelving Team discovered that where the library placed its photocopy machines was almost as critical to some library customers as having the materials returned to the shelf.

Finally, the teams found that some issues they perceived as critical were not seen as such by their customers. For example, the Documents Team was originally formed to examine the flow of documents from receipt in the library to availability on the shelf. However, the survey revealed that the major issue for many documents users was not difficulty in finding the materials, but in finding the location of the Government Publications Unit in the library. Because of this information, the Documents Team shifted its emphasis to developing better location signs and improving interdepartmental training.

Throughout the TQM process, the teams and their sponsor encountered situations which were unforeseen. The Documents Team lost a facilitator in the middle of its work and lost valuable time in finding a new one. Because of scheduling problems, both teams sometimes met without all of the members, resulting in a rehashing of decisions made at earlier meetings. Both teams also met at times without their facilitators, causing either confusion for the team leader, who had to be both a facilitator and a participant, and/or meetings which lacked focus. At any given time, some member of the teams wanted to quit either because the work was taking too much time, or they did not see progress being made. Since none of these things had been discussed during the TQM training, both teams relied heavily on the University TQM Trainer for support and advice.

Both team leaders met regularly with the Assistant University Librarian for Research and Public Services to provide progress reports and discuss successes and failures. At those meetings, they decided to implement some solutions before their final recommendations were prepared. While this improved the immediate work flow, it did skew some of the team's data collection. This was particularly true with the Shelving Team which was formed because shelving was often drastically behind during the first term of the school year and wasn't caught up until the following term. Therefore, when the Shelving Team came up with some simple solutions for improving shelving, they did not want to wait until the team had completed the entire TQM process.

A simple example of this was the team's decision to have shelvers work in groups on assigned floors. Previously, students were sent to shelve on the floors where there was the greatest backlog. In addition, the Stacks Supervisor tried to have shelving coverage for all floors throughout the day. Since the library is open 108 hours a week, this meant that student hours were staggered throughout the day and as a result, student shelvers seldom saw one another. This created a sense of isolation and when the shelving was backlogged, a sense of never catching up. When the TQM team surveyed shelvers, they all commented on this situation. The team used this information to devise a plan which had shelvers working in small groups and each group having an assigned floor. The library lost the benefit of having shelvers working throughout the day, but gained an increased *esprit de corps* among shelvers, tidier shelves and less backlog.

TQM–WHAT HAVE WE LEARNED?

At this point, the library has had two TQM teams meeting for over one year. Both TQM teams have completed their final recommendations to the Assistant University Librarian for Research and Public Services and are implementing them. The Documents Team is addressing two issues which were prominent in their survey. The first, as noted previously, has to do with better directional signs. The Government Publications Unit is located in a difficult-to-find area on the first floor of the library. By ordering larger and easier to read signs, the team anticipates that more people will be able to find the area. The second concern uncovered by the Documents Team was the misinformation some staff and library faculty have about government publications. The documents staff will have a series of training sessions to address this concern. In six month's time, staff from Government Publications will do another user survey to determine if these solutions are addressing the concerns raised in the original survey.

The Shelving Team, too, just completed its final report. As mentioned earlier, the team already began implementation of some of its recommendations and will continue to implement the remaining ones throughout the year. In addition to having teams assigned to each floor, other recommendations include a set of performance standards for shelving, a plan for reorganizing library materials to make the stacks arrangement more sensible, and better training of shelvers in providing information to users in the stacks. The team will work with the recommendations for two terms before doing a new customer survey to see if the changes bring about the anticipated results.

The changes suggested by both TQM teams are indicative of an essential of the TQM process–incremental changes lead to continuous improvement. This fact is also one which causes some library faculty and staff to question whether TQM is worth the time commitment it requires. TQM does not offer a quick solution. Nor, for those who might have been looking for managerial changes, has TQM flattened the library organization. It has moved leadership further down into the organization to the team level which in time, will free up middle managers for more planning and less time putting out brush fires.

TQM is time-consuming, requiring at least three days of training in TQM methodology before it can be used effectively. In addition, each team meets for at least two hours once a week. At Oregon State University Library, both teams have been meeting for a year and are only now concluding their recommendations. Because they were new to the TQM process, more time was spent on flowcharting, preparing the survey and data gathering than would now be required. There is no short cut, and a library contemplating using TQM will want to think of what it will give up in immediate staff productivity in order to accomplish long-range changes. Yet many libraries are similar to the Oregon State University Libraries where the "tendency has been to implement global fixes . . . with no idea which fixes worked or made the most improvement."[4] Moreover, because TQM is predicated on the belief that those who do the work are best able to manage it, it sets the stage for employee participation at all levels of the organization. TQM is "top down" in that it will not be effective in an organization unless those in charge support its implementation. But the tools for change are put into the hands of the team members.

The benefits of TQM for the library and team members are more participation and decision making by those who actually do the work. It has allowed the library, through the customer surveys, to address real concerns of our users and, since TQM emphasizes the ongoing use of performance standards, the library teams will be able to monitor the success of their recommendations.

Oregon, along with many other states, suffers from property tax limitations which make general fund revenues scarce. While TQM cannot solve serious fiscal difficulties, it does provide us with a method for making decisions on how to provide quality services with dwindling resources. Historically, libraries have always taken the lead in providing good customer service and historically, we have also had to do more with less. Libraries must be able to continue to do that which they do best–bringing people and information together. TQM, by providing a method for managing resources effectively can help us do that.

In a year and a half, Oregon State University Libraries' work with TQM is slowly creating a culture which looks at customer service and quality improvement in almost every undertaking. Frequently, when a problem arises, someone will suggest forming a TQM team to study it. TQM is seen by library staff and faculty as an impartial problem-solving tool and one which anyone can use. This is, perhaps, one of the most important benefits of the TQM process.

NOTES

1. Edwin L. Coate. *Total Quality Management at Oregon State* (Corvallis, OR: Oregon State University, 1992), p. 6.
2. The Administration of the Oregon State University Libraries is two-tiered. Library Administration includes the Director of Libraries, the Assistant University Librarian for Research and Public Services, the Assistant University Librarian for Technical and Automation Services and the Administrative Assistant. Division Heads refers to library middle managers who head up the following divisions: Research and Access Services, Reference Services, Special Reference Services, Collection Services and Special Collections, Hatfield Marine Science Center Library, Acquisitions, Cataloging and Library Automation.
3. Ibid., p. 38.
4. Ibid., p. 24.

SUGGESTED SOURCES

Coate, L. Edwin. *Total Quality Management at Oregon State University.* Corvallis, OR: Oregon State University, March 1992.

Drucker, Peter F. "The New Productivity Challenge," *Harvard Business Review* (November-December 1991): 70-79.

Franklin, William H. "Who Cares? Eight Principles for Dealing with Customers," *Exchange* (June 1992): 7-10.

Mackey, Terry & Kitty Mackey. "Think Quality! The Deming Approach *Does* Work in Libraries," *Library Journal* (May 15, 1992): 57-61.

Walters, Jonathan. "The Cult of Total Quality," *Governing* (May 1992): 38-42.

Implementing Total Quality Management: A Model for Research Libraries

Susan B. Barnard

BACKGROUND

This model for implementing total quality management (TQM) in a research library was developed as part of an effort by the Association of Research Libraries' (ARL) Office of Management Services to create strategies and programs for introducing quality improvement approaches in research libraries. The model was presented to a group of ARL directors at the ALA Midwinter Meeting in San Antonio, Texas, January 1992. The group was composed of directors (or their representatives) who had some knowledge of the principles and processes of quality management; some were involved in or anticipating quality initiatives at their own institutions.

A WORD ABOUT MODELS AND IMPLEMENTATION

Gordon L. Lippitt defines a model as "a representation of structures and processes describing in simplified form some aspect of the world."[1] The model presented here illustrates a comprehensive,

Susan B. Barnard is Head of Periodical Information and Access Services (PIAS) at the Kent State University Libraries, Kent, OH.

[Haworth co-indexing entry note]: "Implementing Total Quality Management: A Model for Research Libraries." Barnard, Susan B. Co-published simultaneously in the *Journal of Library Administration,* (The Haworth Press, Inc.) Vol. 18, No. 1/2, 1993, pp. 57-70; and: *Integrating Total Quality Management in a Library Setting* (ed: Susan Jurow, and Susan B. Barnard), The Haworth Press, Inc., 1993, pp. 57-70. Multiple copies of this article/chapter may be purchased from The Haworth Document Delivery Center. Call 1-800-3-HA-WORTH (1-800-342-9678) between 9:00 - 5:00 (EST) and ask for DOCUMENT DELIVERY CENTER.

systematic process of integrating total quality management into a research library environment, beginning with exploration by top management. After the decision to introduce total quality management has been made, the process which follows is commonly referred to as "implementation." However, that term is deceptive for it seems to imply the execution of a task, of yet another program, or the imposition of a totally new and pervasive operational structure. TQM is a process, not a program, a project, or least of all, a quick fix. Undertaking TQM is not a matter of throwing a switch that starts a series of gears into motion.

Nor is TQM simply the latest management fad, likely to be replaced in a year or so by another technique, as some skeptics claim. Just ask the Japanese who have been pursuing this particular "fad" for forty years. Rather, TQM represents a new era of organizational operation which may be ushering in an "age of the customer." In libraries and other service organizations, TQM should be viewed as a means of transition to this new era, and of creating a different framework, one based on proven quality values and practices.

In the case of the manufacturing and corporate sectors where TQM developed, implementation may promote—even require—sudden, holistic change. But, in libraries a more integrative approach is possible. For example, the TQM elements of participative management, staff training and development, and responsive service to users are already established concepts in libraries. As a result, libraries are in a position to expand and improve upon principles they already value and employ, while introducing new approaches to planning, problem solving and envisioning future customer services and needs.

Therefore, in considering this model for "implementing" TQM in research libraries, we may want to think in subtler, yet more profound terms, such as "adopting a total quality approach" or "creating a quality, customer-focused library." Although this model proposes the implementation process in four phases and ten steps, this does not mean that these steps and activities must be strictly sequential, or that all are mandatory. Rather, the model presents the various issues, elements and processes that would comprise a comprehensive TQM-based transition.

Following initial exploration and the decision to adopt quality management, a library may undertake some activities concurrently and others, in a different order, or to a different degree, than is described. Lippitt suggests using models in organizational renewal as "a means of integrating knowledge, providing understanding, and guiding developmental strategies."[2] That is what this model attempts to do.

Finally, the terminology of TQM creates barriers to understanding and acceptance, particularly in academic environments. Neither the term "TQM" nor the theory behind it is monolithic or precise. Such terms as TQM, total quality, quality management, quality improvement, total quality leadership and total customer responsiveness abound, and new ones are being created continually as more organizations, and types of organizations, undertake the transition. Several of these terms are used interchangeably in this article; this serves to broaden the context and emphasize the diversity but common purpose of the language.

PHASE ONE: FIRST STEPS

Step One: Exploration

It is generally agreed and emphatically reiterated that commitment by top management is essential to the lasting success of TQM in any organization. While initial activity may occur elsewhere in an organization and set an example for wider interest and involvement, many practitioners believe that such successes will be limited and short-lived without the support and commitment of top management, and the performance of certain functions by management, as outlined below.

In university libraries, in particular, the question may be, "Who constitutes top management?" Is it the management of the library, the university, the board of trustees, or the state government which provides a significant portion of institutional funding? Leadership and incentive for adopting quality management is often provided by university or state administrations, and this can add political incentive, as well as resources, training and other support, for a library's

TQM effort. However, if these incentives are not present, a library can still create its own quality culture and even provide leadership for other units on campus. In fact, a library is probably one of several good starting points for TQM in a university because it embodies and serves both academic and administrative functions, and is an operation of sufficient size, resources and stature within the institution to provide a good example.

The purpose of the exploration phase is to gather information toward developing a critical mass of knowledge among library managers about total quality management and its potential role and usefulness in their library. Activities may include reading and discussing key books and articles about TQM, particularly on its adaptation in educational and public sector, nonprofit organizations; visiting or working with exemplary companies or institutions which employ quality management, including other departments in the university or other libraries in the state; engaging outside speakers and consultants; and participation of the library director (or dean) and other library managers at conferences, seminars and training sessions sponsored by various quality (and increasingly, library) associations (e.g., GOAL/QPC, Association for Quality and Productivity).

Whoever the provider, initial training seminars should be designed to define quality management; provide brief historical background on the quality movement; review its adaptation in educational and nonprofit organizations; introduce and develop meaningful understanding of key quality principles and processes; outline implementation strategies and plans; and present considerations regarding the decision whether to implement quality management, such as whom to involve in that decision.

Step Two: Decision to Implement/Management Commitment

The purpose of this phase is to build understanding of and support for quality management implementation among top and middle managers and other key library staff. Reasons for reaching the decision to implement TQM should be explained and discussed. Activities may include orientation sessions for all management and key supervisory staff, governance groups, or all library staff, and making resources available to provide further information for those who are interested (e.g., reading lists, articles, and films/videos).

Ample opportunity should be provided for concerns and questions about quality management to be aired and addressed. Strong commitment by top library management to the implementation and continuation of the quality effort must be demonstrated during this phase and throughout the implementation process, particularly if leadership and support are not being provided by the university or larger institution.

PHASE TWO: ORGANIZING FOR QUALITY (PREPARE)

In Phase Two the sequential sense of activities in the initial steps begins to blur, and the limitations of a linear TQM model become evident. On the implementation diagram (Figure 1), three of the primary activities of Phase Two (organizational assessment, understanding customers, and vision and guiding principles) could be subsumed under the fourth, leadership planning. All four are presented concurrently and in no particular order. Movement through these activities might best be perceived as circular, but all are important preparatory activities which, ideally, should be addressed before advancing to Phase Three.

Step Three: Leadership Planning

Ideally, planning for and implementation of quality management should be linked to organizational strategic planning. An organization familiar with articulating its vision and objectives, and with establishing action plans and goals, is well-prepared to incorporate quality principles and procedures into those processes.

Organizational Assessment

Before embarking on a quality management endeavor, a library may want to determine whether and in which ways its cultural environment is, or is not, compatible with quality management.

FIGURE 1

TOTAL QUALITY MANAGEMENT
LIBRARY IMPLEMENTATION MODEL

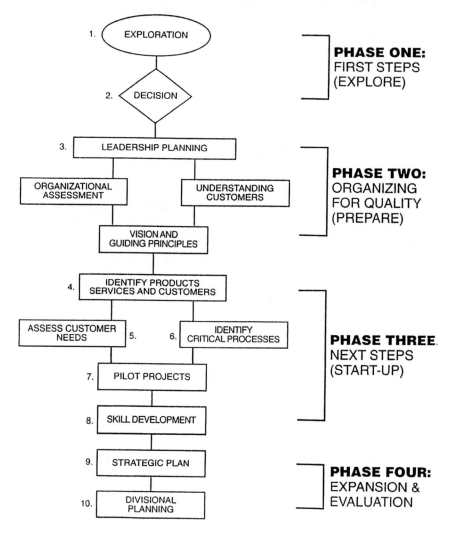

Organizations with total quality cultures have clear values and be-liefs which frame quality processes and foster total quality behav-ior; their environments and operations are relentlessly managed to support those values and beliefs. Peter Linkow defines culture as "the values and beliefs that most members of the organization share; beliefs are assumptions about what is true while values are assumptions about what is worthwhile or desirable."[3]

A number of instruments and methods are available for assessing organizational culture, in general, and organizational readiness to adopt quality management, in particular. Some of these may have to be modified or adapted for use in research libraries. Linkow pre-sents a "Total Quality Culture Matrix" designed to identify current cultural values and targets for cultural change. Another relatively simple and easy-to-use instrument is the "Total Quality Manage-ment Inventory" by Gaylord Reagan.[4] This inventory is designed for individuals at any or all levels of an organization to assess the emphasis the organization places on eight quality criteria: top man-agement leadership and support; strategic planning; customer fo-cus; employee training and recognition; employee empowerment and teamwork; quality measurement and analysis; quality assur-ance; and quality and productivity-improvement results.

A more extensive assessment instrument is the Department of Defense's "Quality and Productivity Self-Assessment Guide for Defense Organizations," designed for use by government agencies. Many corporations use the criteria of the Malcolm Baldrige Nation-al Quality Award (for which only the private sector is eligible) to conduct organizational assessment. Similarly, non-profit organiza-tions may wish to use the "Criteria and Scoring Guidelines for the President's Award for Quality and Productivity Improvement" (for which Federal agencies are eligible), or the set of criteria used for the Quality Improvement Prototype Award (for which smaller orga-nizational units within Federal agencies are eligible).[5]

Understanding Customers

The core of the entire TQM process is understanding customers–external and internal–and relentlessly focusing on customer service and satisfaction. One indicator of the significance of customer service in TQM is the 300-point value assigned to the "customer service" category (out of a possible 1000 points in seven categories) in the rating system for the Malcolm Baldrige Award.

A comprehension of the principles and importance of customer service and satisfaction as a primary goal of quality management is critical for the fullest realization of its potential in libraries. In fact, of all of the elements of quality management, the two which are perhaps least familiar to libraries, yet are potentially the most beneficial aspects, are (1) customer focus and (2) continuous improvement through statistical process control. It is important to place special emphasis on these aspects when libraries pursue quality management.

All senior and middle-level library managers should have customer service and satisfaction awareness training early in the TQM implementation process. A timely schedule of similar training for department heads and all other staff in both public and technical services areas should be established. This could be accomplished with a one- or two-day training seminar which would cover identifying customer expectations, evaluating customer satisfaction, strategies and techniques for improving customer service and satisfaction, and helping staff to improve delivery of services. Comparisons and contrasts between traditional library service concepts and a true customer service focus should be included.

Vision and Guiding Principles

"No matter how good individuals in an organization may be, there has to be a collective vision of what the organization is and wants to be, and some method of assessing individual performance and progress."[6]

Developing a vision and guiding principles helps to create a common understanding among top managers and all other staff about what the library should look like in the future, and what principles will guide the actions they take to achieve that desired future. These agreements will become the basis for formal statements of the organizations' vision and values.

A vision is a clear, positive, forceful statement of what the organization wants to be in three to five, or ten years. A well-crafted vision, supported by concise guiding principles and action, can be a powerful tool for focusing the organization towards a common goal.[7] After the vision statement is completed, barriers to achieving it should be identified. These can then become the basis for developing action plans to deal with the barriers.

PHASE THREE: NEXT STEPS (START-UP)

Step Four: Identifying Products, Services and Customers

Step four serves as a group of related, transitional activities between the planning and organizational activities of Phase Two and the practical applications in Phase Three. These activities include (1) identifying the services and products the library offers; (2) identifying principal external and internal customers and placing them into major groupings (segmentation); and (3) identifying services and products provided to each group of customers. These activities may be accomplished, in conjunction with some activities in Phase Two, at a two-or-three day retreat for senior and middle managers.

Step Five: Assessment of Customer Expectations and Needs

Libraries must not only know who their customers are, they must have a basis for assessing their needs and expectations. Three simple but important principles to keep in mind regarding customers are: (1) the most important part of any organization is its customer; (2) in order to attract new customers and hold old ones you have to satisfy their needs; (3) you can't satisfy their needs unless you know what their needs are.

Building on the results of the management retreat, an assessment of external customer expectations and needs for library services and products should be conducted. This assessment can be carried out by a subcommittee of the full senior/middle management group, or an appointed task force, coordinated by a senior manager.

Tools such as surveys, interviews, customer complaints and feedback, focus groups, or a combination of these may be used. Customer groups may be segmented and surveyed separately (e.g., different surveys for faculty and students). The purpose of the assessment is to determine customer expectations; to assess customer satisfaction with existing services, products and processes; and to identify problem areas and unmet customer needs.

Quality function deployment (QFD) is a strategic tool for identifying and prioritizing customer needs, and then aligning an organization's products and services to meet them. Using QFD, customer needs and the characteristics of a service system can be placed in a matrix and compared. The subcommittee or task force may then make recommendations on how the organization can address unmet customer needs or otherwise improve customer satisfaction.

Another task force or subcommittee may also be formed to assess internal customer needs and expectations. Or, all departments may engage in identifying their own internal customers and their respective needs and/or expectations.

Step Six: Identifying and Measuring Critical Processes

Every organization is made up of separate but usually interrelated processes which help determine how work is organized and how customer needs are met. A process is "a flow of work that progresses from one person or one activity to another." A critical process is "an important process, defined by customer need, that is a major part of the mission of the organization." Identifying and evaluating the critical processes that drive an organization is vital to the continuous improvement of systems fundamental to TQM.

Using the subcommittee/task force results, the full senior/middle level management group might, in a second retreat, identify a maximum of ten of the library's "critical processes" (i.e., those processes that are necessary to the long-term functioning of the organization and its ability to meet customer needs). For each critical process, one or two ways of measuring progress over time (i.e., strategic indicators) will be defined. Organizational flowcharting or critical process charting can facilitate these activities.

The management group will then select several critical processes wherein pilot projects could be conducted. One or two processes directly benefitting external customers, and one benefitting internal customers might be chosen. In selecting processes for pilot projects consideration should be given to:

- importance of the process to primary customers;
- whether the process is experiencing difficulty and is recognized as needing attention;
- likelihood of eliminating waste (by saving money, staff time, etc.).

In other words, the pilot project process should be important to the organization and have a good chance of succeeding. A popular way of expressing this is to "pick fruit that is closest to the ground."

Step Seven: Initial Pilot Project Teams

Initial pilot project teams ("quality teams") are formed to involve staff from various levels of the library in the quality management process, and to create organization-wide participation in problem-solving. Teams are created to address specific issues and critical processes that have been targeted for improvement. Teams meet on a regular basis and use a structured, problem-solving system to identify issues, gather and analyze data, and develop solutions (see Constance Towler's article on team training in this volume). The team must agree to and abide by certain operating guidelines.

A quality team is formed for each pilot project. Teams are usually composed of no more than ten members, all of whom are major owners of the process (e.g., anyone who works on any part of the process, regardless of rank). Each team has: a sponsor; a facilitator; a team leader; and team members. The role of each participant is known and clearly defined:

Sponsor–usually the highest level manager of the organizational unit that controls the process. He or she is not on the team but approves the results of and signs off on each action step taken by the team.

Facilitator–from another department than that where the process being studied resides; therefore, is not expected to have the content knowledge which the team has. He or she is the owner of the TQM problem-solving model, teaches the team how to use the various TQM tools, and assists team members in communicating with each other and in coming to decisions.

Team Leader–the supervisor responsible for the performance of the selected critical process. He or she has three primary roles: (1) information path between the team and the sponsor/management; (2) logistics coordinator (e.g., scheduling team meetings, keeping team records, etc.); and (3) implementor and evaluator of the team and its procedures (with facilitator).

Team Members–owners of an identified process, anyone who works on any part of the process, regardless of their status in the organization. Team members participate fully in team meetings and activities.

Step Eight: Team Member Skill Development

Sponsors, facilitators and all members of the pilot teams undergo quality team training. Sponsors, facilitators, team leaders and TQM trainer (three people for each team plus alternate facilitators and team leaders and a trainer or trainers; a total of at least eleven for two teams) will attend workshops on meeting management (two hours), team leader training (one day), and facilitator training (one to two days). All team participants will attend workshops on interactive skills (three hours), consensus decision-making (one hour), and the problem-solving process (two days).

The problem-solving process is perhaps the most important aspect of team training and team dynamics as it is the blueprint according to which teams conduct their work. The problem-solving model accomplishes three objectives: develops among all team members a clear, shared understanding of the issues; provides for a detailed assessment of customer requirements; drives solutions by fact by prescribing data analysis methods and measurement tools.

PHASE FOUR: EVALUATION AND EXPANSION

In Phase Four the quality improvement approach becomes integrated into all library operations and quality values, understood by all library staff. The results of the pilot projects are evaluated and presented to all library staff, and suggestions are made for improvements in the problem-solving process and team training. New teams and cross-functional teams will be formed to advance skill development among larger numbers of staff and to undertake other important quality improvement projects. Quality orientation and training is extended to all new staff. Steps nine and ten are two further activities which promote this integration.

Step Nine: Creating a TQM Strategic Plan

Senior management will create a three to five-year TQM master plan, focusing on key breakthrough issues and improvement targets. Earlier efforts to identify products, services and customers, and to identify customer needs may need to be reviewed and modified. In creating this plan, a one-year plan is made with goals that can be targeted for immediate attention in the first year. Beyond the first year, the rest of the five-year plan involves adopting TQM policies at all levels of the organization. Library-wide TQM activities will be outlined and carried out.

Step Ten: Divisional/Departmental Planning

Divisional and departmental planning will take place, reflecting key systems or functions targeted for improvement in the strategic plan. Each manager or supervisor will identify one or two breakthrough objectives to achieve the targeted objectives of the strategic plan.

Recognition and rewards programs should be initiated to highlight successful projects, teams and efforts. Upcoming projects will be selected and communicated throughout the library.

CONCLUSION

Eight years after he introduced quality management at the Corning corporation, CEO James Houghton was asked if he would have done anything differently; he replied that he wished he had initiated TQM in 1953 instead of 1983. He also said he would have had the company focus on external customers sooner than it did (internal customers were addressed in phase one of their effort and external customers, in phase two). Houghton's description of his experience with quality management can serve as an example and a reassurance to library managers contemplating the quality journey. He said, "When I got into this I hadn't a clue that it would be this important. I just held my nose and jumped in."[8]

NOTES

This model is based primarily on the following materials:

"Total Quality Management: Ten Elements for Implementation" (GOAL/ QPC, Methuen, MA); "How to Get Started Implementing Total Quality Management" (cited below); and "Implementing Total Quality Management in a University Setting" (by Edwin L. Coate, Oregon State University, Corvallis, Oregon). It also draws upon materials from the University of Wisconsin, Madison, the Harvard Quality Process (Harvard University), and a variety of other sources which address quality management in private and public sector organizations.

1. Gordon L. Lippitt, *Organizational Renewal: A Holistic Approach to Organizational Development.* 2nd ed. (Englewood Cliffs, NJ: Prentice-Hall, Inc. 1982), p. xiv.

2. Ibid., p. 400.

3. Peter Linkow, "Is Your Culture Ready for Total Quality?" Quality Progress (November 1989).

4. Gaylord Reagan, "Total Quality Management (TQM) Inventory," *The 1992 Annual: Developing Human Resources.* (San Diego, CA: Pfeiffer & Company, 1992).

5. The instruments cited here are recommended in the Federal Quality Institute's *How to Get Started Implementing Total Quality Management,* part of the Federal Total Quality Management Handbook series (Washington, D.C.: U.S. Government Printing Office, June 1990).

6. Daryl Anderson, State of Minnesota Pollution Control Agency. Remarks on "Minnesota's Quality Initiative," delivered at the Eighth Annual Conference of GOAL/QPC, Boston, MA, November 12, 1991.

7. *How to Get Started Implementing Total Quality Management.*, p. 10.

8. James Houghton, CEO of Corning Incorporated, speaking at the Eighth Annual Conference of GOAL/QPC, Boston, MA, November 12, 1991.

IMPLEMENTING A TOTAL QUALITY MANAGEMENT PROGRAM

Customer Service:
Another Side of TQM

Arlene Farber Sirkin

The gurus of total quality management ("TQM")–Deming, Juran, and Crosby–differ considerably on strategies and tactics. However, the one common underlying element is satisfaction of the customer. Most of the early work in TQM was based on the manufacturing sector, where quality was translated into no defects in the manufactured product. A product that is defective is not only expensive to replace, but leads to unhappy customers. Too many unhappy customers (because of defective products), leads to too few customers. Just think about the reputations of Japanese cars and American cars.

Arlene Farber Sirkin is President of the Washington Resource Consulting Group, Inc., Washington, DC.

[Haworth co-indexing entry note]: "Customer Service: Another Side of TQM." Sirkin, Arlene Farber. Co-published simultaneously in the *Journal of Library Administration,* (The Haworth Press, Inc.) Vol. 18, No. 1/2, 1993, pp. 71-83; and: *Integrating Total Quality Management in a Library Setting* (ed: Susan Jurow, and Susan B. Barnard), The Haworth Press, Inc., 1993, pp. 71-83. Multiple copies of this article/chapter may be purchased from The Haworth Document Delivery Center. Call 1-800-3-HAWORTH (1-800-342-9678) between 9:00 - 5:00 (EST) and ask for DOCUMENT DELIVERY CENTER.

In translating the concepts and goals of TQM from the management sector to the service sector, the focus remains on customer satisfaction. Like the defective product, defective customer service leads to unhappy customers.

Libraries have competitors, whether that competitor is another library or competition for dollars and staffing within an organization. Unsatisfied customers eventually mean problems for librarians. This article is intended to promote understanding of what makes a satisfied customer.

One need not believe that the customer is always right one hundred percent of the time or that all customers can be satisfied. Some customers will complain that you splash when you walk on water. Others will assume you walk on water because you cannot swim. But for the vast majority of customers a little attention to customer service will go a long way toward customer satisfaction.

WHO IS THE CUSTOMER?

When I first started using the term "customer" many years ago, librarians would complain that they did not have customers. After all, they were not selling used cars or clothes. They had "users" or "patrons." Although "patron service" and "patron satisfaction" certainly could be addressed, it is important to continue to use the term "customer." The "customer" problems of libraries have more in common with the "customer" problems of other businesses than librarians like to think.

A library patron or user is a customer. He or she is demanding a service and expects that service. Whether the library is an academic or public library, the patron may not be directly paying for use of the library, but he or she feels entitled to the service because he or she pays school fees or taxes. Just think about the complaints which arise when libraries cut back hours or services. People complain because they feel that they are being denied a service to which they are entitled.

Similarly, the library of a law firm or business has its customers who expect a certain level of service. If they do not get that service, they will target corporate resources elsewhere to acquire what they need (or acquire new librarians).

Even other librarians and other staff in the library/information center are customers. Often the librarian who provides services directly to the users is a "customer" of other staff members who work behind the scene, because he or she is dependent on the services of those other staff.

WHAT IS CUSTOMER SATISFACTION?

The standard definitions of customer satisfaction include the following elements: repeat customers, referrals or endorsements, meeting (or exceeding) customer expectations, creation of a service-oriented environment.

Many companies and the popular press have jumped on TQM as the current, favored management tool that will revolutionize the workplace. This is unfortunate. Customer satisfaction, which is one aspect of TQM, is a valuable management goal, as companies as diverse as Federal Express, American Express, and Nordstrom's have demonstrated. But it is not something that a company (or a library) can simply initiate by telling its staff to do it. It takes a lot of work and perseverance.

Despite customer satisfaction now appearing under the auspices of TQM, and the popular press's recent fascination with the concept, many of the theories and techniques have been around for years. When I was a librarian at the University of Maryland in the 1970's, I took a course on dealing with difficult patrons. Although it was not called customer satisfaction, that is what it was.

In fact, it seems that most of customer satisfaction is simple, common sense. Indeed, respondents to a Gallup survey on what quality-in-service means suggested: courtesy, attitude, helpfulness, and being treated with respect. However, while common sense can indicate the elements of customer satisfaction, it is much harder to get staff to apply their common sense in day-to-day dealings with customers.

The problem is not that the information and techniques are lacking, but that until recently librarians were not expected to work at it. And despite the common sense elements of customer satisfaction, it takes work to apply common sense to the everyday work environment, especially in this time of limited resources.

Libraries must choose how to spend their limited staff time and funds. In the case of customer satisfaction, these limitations are translated into making sure that customers' expectations are not beyond the library's capacity to deliver.

CUSTOMER EXPECTATIONS

Generally, customers, as well as those nonusers who should be customers, do not have a good idea of what a librarian does and the services a library offers. In a variety of research projects, library customers have been asked what they thought librarians did. The most frequent answers were: checkout books, shelve books, and read books (that would be nice). Those patrons seemingly had trouble differentiating between librarians and library support staff; or perhaps the library had simply created such low expectations of what it offered, no one expected anything more than clerical duties.

One way to view customer expectations is to substitute the concept of customer demand. In simple economic terms, the idea is to supply what it is that the customers demand. If a library supplies something that is not in demand, customers will place very little value on it.

Imagine a game show. The participants get to buy one of three prizes. Prize number 1 is the world's greatest slide rule. The slide rule has been certified by the International Slide Rule Association as the ultimate slide rule. And even more amazingly, it is priced at only $10. Prize number 2 is the world's greatest buggy whip. It has been certified by the International Buggy Whip Society as the ultimate buggy whip. It also is priced at $10. Prize number 3 is a notebook computer. It is priced at $1000.

As you might expect, most in the audience say that they would buy prize number 3, even though it is the most expensive, and would pass on prizes number 1 and 2, even though they are better bargains. The reason is that they can use the computer, but they have no use for the slide rule or buggy whip.

CREATING FALSE EXPECTATIONS

Libraries must be careful not to create false expectations. Libraries are limited by staff, budget, and other resources in what they can do for customers. A customer may not be delighted if he is told that the library cannot provide what he needs, but he is going to be a lot happier about that than if he is promised a service or product which the library cannot deliver.

When I conduct seminars, I ask participants to tell me their expectations for the seminar, either issues listed on the handouts on which they would like me to focus, or issues not specified on the handouts. After what is usually a lively discussion, I ask for a show of hands of those who have spoken. I then give $1 bills (real ones) to all who have participated by making a suggestion, except one person. The audience immediately tells me that I forgot to give a $1 bill to the forgotten person. My question to them is "Did I promise to give everyone who spoke a $1 bill?" The answer is NO. However, by my behavior, I had created an expectation that everyone who participated would get $1.

The catch 22 is that by delivering excellent, timely service, libraries create an expectation for the customers. If events happen that prevent meeting that expectation, such as reductions in staff, or even a one-time occurrence, such as staff being out sick, we need to inform the customer and change their expectations.

Think about the household repairman for whom the customer had to take off from work. Companies will say that the repairman will be there in the morning or afternoon, but rarely will they give an estimated time. They do not want to create false expectations. If he actually shows up in the morning, even if it is 11:55, the customer's expectations have been met. However, if the company had said he would probably be there around 10 a.m., and he showed up at 11:55, the customer would be upset (even if they called to say he was delayed).

Libraries must achieve that careful balance between customers who expect too much and customers who expect too little. Both can be made into satisfied customers if the customer understands the library's limitations up-front and the librarian understands the customer's needs and expectations up-front.

HOW ARE CUSTOMER EXPECTATIONS DETERMINED?

Determining customer expectations is to some extent a lot simpler than meeting customer expectations; librarians should simply ask running focus groups and conducting user surveys to determine customer expectations help. But a good starting point before going through that methodology is simply to ask customers what they find useful.

As obvious as it seems, some librarians do not recognize that customers determine customer expectations. Librarians can provide information that will affect those expectations, but it is the customer who forms the expectations. Although this seems simple, too often librarians say: "We offered this service and no one is using it. Don't they realize how wonderful this is?" Library staff may feel that it is unfair that their best ideas are not utilized. They feel they as library staff know what the users (or nonusers) need. (Of course, the problem may simply be that a customer cannot be expected to want something, or expect the library to deliver it, if they do not know that it is available, or if they do not understand what it is.)

Some time ago, I did a market research project for a special library in a scientific setting. They had a rule that they would respond to all inquiries within 24 hours. When we asked the customers if they valued this (*i.e.,* did they always need the answer in 24 hours), we found that many of them did not need the information that quickly. By asking when the information was needed, we were able to define and then meet the customers' expectations (as well as make life easier for the staff).

Sometimes other sections of the library or of the business are a useful source of feedback. Most people do not like to give bad news. Many people will just go elsewhere rather than complain about poor service. Sometimes customers will complain to someone in a related department. Thus, the reference section might hear criticisms of circulation, and vice versa. It is critical that a system be in place to solicit this feedback and make sure it gets back to the appropriate department.

In conducting in-house training sessions for staff of large library systems, the staff members sometimes do not really know each other or understand what other departmental staff do, although they frequently offer related services and should consider themselves part of a team. Instead, they view themselves as rivals for limited dollars or limited customers. Hopefully, after discussing services across departmental lines, the staff recognizes how they can help each other, and thus help the customer. They recognize that instead of competing for scarce customers, by working together they can better serve their customers and eventually expand their customer base.

Focus groups are also an excellent way to determine customer expectations and address them, especially if the library wishes to target specific groups. One major urban library was concerned about underuse by teenagers. They determined by use of focus groups that most teenagers considered librarians "nerds" and libraries a place where only "nerds" went. With that in mind, the library worked with some students and teachers to change that image.

Other libraries have conducted focus groups with, and to determine the needs of, the physically impaired, the art community, local businesses, senior citizens, working parents, parents of small children, specific ethnic populations, and teachers. The Library of Congress recently conducted focus groups with Congressional staffers to get feedback about their services and products. Often a special library will target a unit or department which it feels it can help, but which is underutilizing the library's services. For example, an academic library may realize that they never see any members of a particular department and need to focus on finding out why this department is not using its services. Where are they getting their information? Are there barriers either geographic, or other that are interfering? What do the faculty and researchers in this department need from their library?

COMPLAINT SYSTEMS

One of the underused techniques of determining customer expectations and satisfaction is a complaint system. Often libraries either do not have such a system or the system is underutilized. In many cases, staff handles the problem without a log or some other way to track the complaints. Thus, repetitive problems, such as the lack of effective signs, never get solved. According to the U.S. Office of Consumer Affairs, each complaint on average represents twenty-seven others that do not get reported. In some cases, people do not say what they mean and only by probing can the issue be identified. Often the simple fact that library staff listen and explain what the situation is, and why the library cannot resolve their problems will keep them as customers. Remember it is not only what the library staff does, but how the library handles customers, that is important.

Recently, the following complaints and responses were posted on a bulletin board at the Halifax, Nova Scotia Public Library:

> Comment: The section with the Greek books is very high. Your average Greek person is between 5'-2" to 5'-5". Wouldn't it be better if the books were placed in the lower shelves? Suggestion: Perhaps switch around with the German, after all it is only a very small rearrangement alphabetically. Thank you.

> Reply: But what do we tell the short Germans? Seriously, help is at hand or, anyway, at foot. There are five kick-stools in the non-fiction area. They are on rollers, so just kick one along the multilingual shelves and rise (two steps) above hoi polloi.

> Comment: The Ongoing and Unsolved Problem of the Homeless in the Library. Today someone has spilled caramel popcorn all over the rug in the magazine section. A man is sleeping in the magazine section, blocking access to the racks. Last week a man was eating chips and they were all over the rug. The Salvation Army says that there is adequate shelter and food available for our homeless. Therefore, I see no reason why they should use the library as a boarding house.

> Reply: Many of the homeless people who come here are regular library patrons who (lacking a permanent address) do not have library cards, but enjoy access to our newspaper and magazine collections. However, no one should be eating or sleeping on the premises: if you note people doing either, please draw it to our attention. Our security officer is aware of local services and has been able to put many homeless patrons in touch with appropriate services. We will try to keep a closer

eye on the reading room, and remind patrons that they must not bring food there.

IT IS IMPORTANT TO KEEP CUSTOMERS

Most librarians are already working very hard. Why then should they worry about their customers' expectations? One obvious reason is that if the library has no customers, it loses its justification for funding and, sadly, some libraries are facing sizable reductions or outright closings.

One statistic often cited is that it is on average five to fifteen times harder to get a new customer than to keep an existing one. This will vary by industry. The figures for libraries are unknown, but the point is clear. It is a lot easier to satisfy the person who already is in the library, than it is to get new customers to come to the library.

As a starting point, libraries should focus their efforts on their existing customers. The idea is that it is important to provide excellent service to existing customers, instead of devoting too many resources to getting new customers. Those who know the library and how the facility works should be easier to work with since they already understand the system. Word of mouth is still one of the best forms of advertising, particularly in a closed environment such as a special library. Satisfied customers bring new customers. Dissatisfied customers discourage new and existing customers.

Many customers do not complain before they leave, they just leave. But, they frequently tell their friends about their bad experience. Studies have shown that a dissatisfied customer on average tells twice as many people as a satisfied customer. People seem to love to complain to their friends. The bottom line is that all of the major causes of customer dissatisfaction are strongly linked to human performance. Therefore, an organization's staff has the greatest impact on the satisfaction of its customers.

EMPOWERMENT

One term that often comes up when an organization starts focusing on customer service is empowerment. This basically entails giving responsibility and authority to those doing the tasks for the evaluation and improvement of the areas where they work. Most organizations find, if properly implemented, that this generates increased commitment and loyalty on the part of staff because they are given an increased stake in the results. Yet, to do this effectively, the staff needs specific skill training in areas such as dealing with difficult people, problem solving, and team building. This requires an investment of time for training and for meetings.

YOU CANNOT SATISFY ALL OF THE PEOPLE ALL OF THE TIME

A consultant recently received back evaluations from one of her seminars. On the feedback form it specifically asked how the course could be improved. The first two responses were both complimentary, but under "how to improve" one said "should be *more* interactive," and the second, "should be *less* interactive." The course description clearly said that the course had both lecture and interactive sessions. It delivered exactly what was promised (and, based on the other evaluations, what was expected), yet these two participants' expectations of what "interactive" meant in the course brochure were quite different. With customers, you cannot always win.

CONCLUSION

Improved customer service and satisfaction is a long-term strategic initiative. As outlined above, it requires a commitment of time and money to provide training, to allow time for staff to meet, to focus and brainstorm, and to get feedback from customers. This will be most effective if there is commitment from the head of the organization, not only of funds and time, but as a role model. This is a hard period for libraries, whether special (e.g., academic or corporate), or public. A strategic focus on customer service and satisfaction is an effective tool to help libraries accomplish their mission.

SELECTED SOURCES

Albrecht, Karl and Ron Zemke, *Service America: Doing Business in the New Economy* (Homewood, Ill.: Dow Jones-Irwin, 1985).

Rosabeth Moss Kanter, *The Change Masters* (New York: Simon and Schuster, 1983).

Lele, Milind M. and Jagdish N. Sheth, *The Customer is Key* (New York: John Wiley, 1987).

Zeithaml, Valarie A., A. Parasuraman, and Leonard L. Berry, *Delivering Quality Service: Balancing Customers' Perceptions and Expectations* (New York: The Free Press, 1990).

Goodman, John, Arlene Malech, and Colin Adamson, "Don't Fix the Product, Fix the Customer," *Quality Review* (Fall 1988), European edition, pp.6-11.

Block, Peter. *The Empowered Manager.* San Francisco: Jossey-Bass, 1987.

APPENDIX I

WHAT ARE ORGANIZATIONS DOING TO IMPROVE CUSTOMER SERVICE AND SATISFACTION?

Some of the key things that organizations are doing to improve customer service and satisfaction ("css") are the following:

- Preparing mission statements that include customer service and satisfaction
- Conducting css skill training
- Running css-focused new employee orientation
- Conducting css systems/technology review
- Doing a css practices/policies audit
- Holding senior management meetings on css
- Developing a css slogan
- Implementing a reward/recognition system based on css performance
- Having organization-wide css communications
- Developing css standards
- Getting feedback from customers

Of the items listed above, the mission statement and senior management meetings on css are most widely implemented. Yet these are cited least as being effective because they do not reach those in the trenches. For those same reasons, css skill training, reward recognition systems and feedback from customers are the most effective strategies.

APPENDIX II

WHAT ARE SOME WAYS LIBRARY/INFORMATION CENTERS HAVE IMPROVED CUSTOMER SERVICE AND SATISFACTION?

The following is a list of some of the methods that libraries have identified to improve customer service and satisfaction ("css"). The list is not exhaustive. It includes ideas both from special and public libraries.

- Provide service brochure for new patrons
- Improve signs–external and internal
- Change (extend) hours
- Allow videos to be returned in bookdrop
- Have simplified checkout of audio cassettes
- Have portable phone available for staff in stacks
- Prepare information kits on hot topics
- Train patrons how to use the library
- Conduct a survey on what inhibits service
- Use E-mail
- Crosstrain staff
- Open satellite offices
- Flexibility in staff assignments
- Focus on customers' and staff's needs
- Work on better cooperation with local government
- Have vendors give demonstrations of online systems, etc.
- Give new staff a better orientation
- Adopt a shelf program (shelf read)
- Create library advisory groups from each department
- Hold a "stump the librarian" day
- Add css to staff job descriptions
- Do better planning of the physical layout
- Conduct and follow-up on surveys
- Create a form for tracking complaints
- Have an active outreach program
- Create a videotape explaining the library
- Publicize downsizing, changes

- Reprioritize jobs
- Develop training materials
- Target services to specific groups
- Offer electronic document delivery
- Offer more bibliographies–for targeted groups
- Provide a list of library services and contact people
- Smile

TQM Training:
The Library Service Challenge

Tim Loney
Arnie Bellefontaine

TQM, an outgrowth of private sector experience, is increasingly making inroads into the public and non-profit sectors. This expansion into the public sector is not without controversy.[1] One of the cornerstones of TQM is the focus on the customer. Defining the customer in the public sector can be a complex and politically sensitive activity. One of the challenges can be the competing needs of customers. An example in the library community is clients with contradictory demands, e.g., those who would like access to *Playboy* in their local library branch and those who do not think it should be in their library.[2] Notwithstanding these complications, there are library patrons who have clear and noncontroversial needs that can be fully satisfied.

The notion of customer is certainly not a foreign concept to anyone working in the library community. In a paper prepared for

---

Tim Loney is currently Regional Quality Manager for the U.S. General Services Administration (GSA). He is Professor and Research Advisor in the Human Resource Organization Development Division at the University of San Francisco. Arnie Bellefontaine is TQM Trainer with the U.S. General Services Administration and a former executive officer at the Library of Congress.

[Haworth co-indexing entry note]: "TQM Training: The Library Service Challenge." Loney, Tim, and Arnie Bellefontaine. Co-published simultaneously in the *Journal of Library Administration,* (The Haworth Press, Inc.) Vol. 18, No. 1/2, 1993, pp. 85-95; and: *Integrating Total Quality Management in a Library Setting* (ed: Susan Jurow, and Susan B. Barnard), The Haworth Press, Inc., 1993, pp. 85-95. Multiple copies of this article/chapter may be purchased from The Haworth Document Delivery Center. Call 1-800-3-HAWORTH (1-800-342-9678) between 9:00 - 5:00 (EST) and ask for DOCUMENT DELIVERY CENTER.

the 1992 midwinter meeting of the American Library Association (ALA), Susan Barnard reports that a "comprehension of the principles and importance of customer service and satisfaction as a primary goal of quality management is critical for the fullest realization of its potential in libraries."[3]

The notion of service to a client is firmly embedded in the efficacy of the library function. More significantly, service is critical to the survival of the library community. A major underlying impetus for adopting TQM processes in the private sector has been competition and survival. Yet, in the public sector, it is hard to appreciate the notion of competition, since we typically envision government entities as being sole providers of unique services. Not so for libraries, for which changes in technology have made it possible for private information vendors to compete in significant ways with libraries. A recent *Business Week* lead article describes how the text of Shakespeare's "Othello" can be reduced to a series of electrical impulses flickering on a personal computer screen.[4]

The intent of this article is not to dwell on the importance of the customer, per se; rather, our focus is on the training and skill requirements in implementing a quality customer service plan. And since the training implications of a quality process are multifaceted and varied, depending on the stage of a quality initiative, training will be addressed in the context of organizing and implementing a quality management initiative.

It might be useful to digress and explain the multifaceted implications of training in the context of the library community. While a service focus currently exists in the library community, this service focus takes on a wholly new meaning in relation to TQM. In a TQM environment, the service focus is not simply an isolated or separate activity or event, rather, *it is an integral part of the entire organization process for accomplishing work and achieving objectives.* For example, the way service is viewed and valued has profound implications on the selection of inputs, on how processes are set up for transforming inputs into outputs, and so on. In other words, service is carefully integrated into the systems dimension of organization activity.

To understand and appreciate the systems dimension of TQM, we are borrowing from the model that Susan Barnard presented at the 1992 ALA midwinter meeting (see Figure 1).[5] The model has been

FIGURE 1

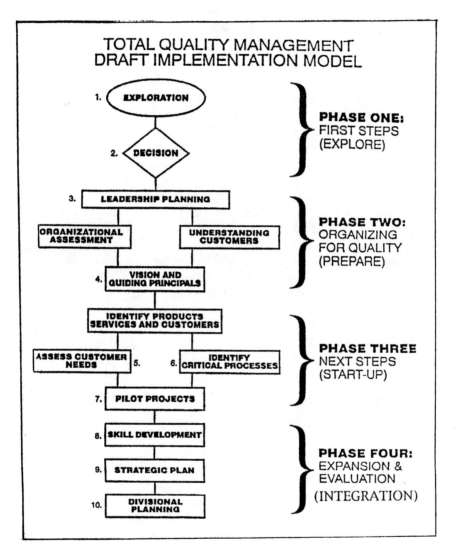

slightly modified to clarify that phase four encompasses the integration of TQM in all work activities as part of the routine way of doing business. Phase three, for example, contains a number of ad hoc activities to evaluate current processes (the old paradigm) and to identify changes to be made to bring the organization in synch with principles of TQM. Kenneth Johnston of Kaset International refers to these ad hoc structures as part of the shadow organization; that is, structures superimposed on the existing (primary) structure.[6] These are typically improvement teams, cross functional groups, and autonomous work units that process assignments in a different manner than traditional work units. In phase four we would expect these shadow organizations to become the primary structures for conducting business.

In terms of the model, it is the authors' contention that there are customer and service implications in each phase, as well as in every step of the model. The fact that "customer" is used in only three steps or boxes in Figure 1 should not detract from the profound implication of customer service. Customer service is a critical issue in deciding to commit to TQM, in the shape of the strategic plan (including the vision statement), and in the training of employees.

Below, the customer service implication of each phase, as well as the relevant training or skill implications, are described. With regard to the latter, the appropriate training requirements of each phase have been summarized in Figure 2. It should be pointed out that there is nothing absolute about the TQM phases described in the model. In fact, in the real world a number of activities in one phase will typically overlap with another phase. Training, too, can overlap from one phase to another.

PHASE ONE–EXPLORATION AND COMMITMENT

During this phase of implementation senior management develops a preliminary understanding of the quality process. This occurs either through attendance at outside (public) seminars and workshops, reading books and other materials, and/or visiting exemplary quality organizations. Another alternative for learning is to arrange for an in-house workshop and having speakers and experts brought in to the organization. Ideally, at least one to two days of such a workshop should be devoted to an overview of the quality manage-

FIGURE 2

PHASE ONE - EXPLORATION AND COMMITMENT

- TQM Awareness/Overview
- Orientation to Quality Customer Service
- "Futures Seminars"
- Quality Conferences
- Site Visits
- Barriers to Change

PHASE TWO - ORGANIZING FOR QUALITY

- Leading the Quality/Service Effort
- Teambuilding for Senior Staff
- Strategic Planning and Visioning
- Orientation to the Gurus (Quality, Service)
- Quality/Customer Assessment
- Benchmarking

PHASE THREE - START UP

- Teambuilding for Team Members
- Quality Tools for Team Members
- Basic Facilitator Development
- Customer Satisfaction
- Client Survey Techniques
- Team Leader Skills

PHASE FOUR - EXPANSION AND INTEGRATION

- Customer Focus Tools and Techniques
- Client Relations Training
- Service Management (Managers/Supervisors)
- Teambuilding
- Exceeding Customer Expectations
- Conducting Service Audits

ment process, including presentations by senior managers of exemplary organizations.

Either as part of this phase or at the outset of phase two, senior staff should have an exposure to the latest developments in customer service relations. This would typically include an understanding of the nature and importance of having a service strategy, cycles of service, barriers to quality service, moments of truth, the importance of empowering front line employees, and setting customer expectations. It would be appropriate to distinguish core services (basic deliverables to the client) and customer services (the interaction with the client).[7]

All of the activities described above are intended to give senior managers the knowledge necessary in making a decision to commit to quality management. In this regard, it might be appropriate to go beyond simply an education on quality and customer service dynamics. In conjunction with considering the possibility of TQM, which is a major change effort, it might be useful to arrange a seminar exploring the implications of current technological developments and other macro-societal changes that either inhibit or potentially enhance the growth of the library community. This activity could provide significant enlightenment on sources of an expanded client base. At this time it might also be appropriate to conduct training on the implications of organization change, in general, and potential barriers precluding a successful change effort.

PHASE TWO–ORGANIZING FOR QUALITY

During this phase, management begins its initial structuring for TQM. Critical to this phase is senior management learning to operate as a team (e.g., a management council or steering committee). Other important activities during this phase include clarifying the customer dimension (internal customer, external customer, primary customers, secondary customers, etc.), assessing current quality and customer service activities, benchmarking best practices, and establishing mission, vision, values, and strategy. This would also be the time for senior management to decide on how to structure TQM; for example, through a steering committee, quality council, full-time or part-time personnel devoted to quality/customer matters, use of consultants, or one of various TQM methodologies (e.g., the approach of Deming, Juran, Crosby, or other "gurus," or more generic approaches).

If senior management has not been previously trained or had extensive experience operating on a team, this would be the place for team training. This would include, among other things, knowledge of team stages, mechanics of meetings, interpersonal skills, valuing differences (e.g., using the Myers-Briggs Type Indicator (MBTI) instrument), and basic problem-solving skills. Depending upon the extent of quality and customer service awareness training provided in phase one, this may be the time for more extensive awareness training, including more detailed exposure to various TQM approaches (i.e., Deming, Juran, Crosby, and others). Training on vision development and strategic planning would also be appropriate. This could be accomplished in a three to five day workshop which would include the development of a preliminary strategy and vision statement, as well as an organization structure for TQM implementation. Such a workshop should be facilitated by an "outside expert." If a particular "guru" approach and/or a major quality management consulting firm is selected, this workshop is likely to be facilitated by a member of their staff.

Prior to this workshop, it would be appropriate to have someone–ideally, an outsider experienced in evaluation or survey techniques–conduct a readiness evaluation. For example, a management climate survey, employee opinion survey or internal client survey might be appropriate. Results of this survey could then be presented at a workshop. If internal personnel are used to conduct the survey and evaluate the data, they should receive appropriate training in such techniques.

Having made the commitment to TQM and the decision on the TQM methodology and structure, quality/service awareness training should be given to all employees. This training should include an explanation from senior management of reasons for the initiative, and what to expect in the coming months.

PHASE THREE–START UP

Phase three involves an intensive evaluation of current work processes and the relationship of these processes to customer needs and expectations. Critical to an effective quality process are (1) thorough identification of customers, (2) their "principal service expectations," and (3) a detailed analysis of key work processes (and specifically, the processes that deliver the services). To the extent that desired outcomes are not being achieved, this is the time to get as close as possible to the root causes precluding achievement of stated goals, as well as setting new service standards.[8]

Resource limitations will preclude simultaneous evaluation of every work process. Decisions will have to be made on which processes to start with; for example, processes that have the most critical impact on customers, are doable in a reasonable period of time, and so on.

Given the heavy emphasis on team activity during this phase, team and quality tools training is critical. Tools should include basic problem solving, voting techniques, brainstorming, flow charting and fishbone diagrams. Team members will need extensive training on the customer service dimension of the quality process, including how customers judge services (e.g., reliability, responsiveness, assurance, empathy).[9] To the extent that team members will be used to solicit information from clients, they will need training in customer satisfaction feedback systems, including skills in developing questionnaires, focus group techniques, mail surveys, listening and conducting interviews.[10]

PHASE FOUR–EXPANSION AND INTEGRATION

During phase four the transition to TQM as the primary way of conducting activity further evolves. The work of the teams in phase three should now be incorporated into organization processes and work activities. As appropriate, new teams will be formed to further refine processes. Senior management will continually monitor and reevaluate progress, including modifications to the strategy as appropriate. At this point the notion of continuous improvement ("Kaizen") should be strongly ingrained in all behaviors. As Wagenheim and Reurink note, "customer needs constantly change and an organization must take responsibility for tracking these changes. Gathering information from the customer should be continuous, formal, and active."[11]

Training in this phase can be extensive. New employees will need awareness training on quality and customer satisfaction, orientation to the strategy and vision, and, as appropriate, training in teambuilding and quality tools skills. New supervisors and managers will need training in quality and customer service awareness, teambuilding and quality tools, and leading the quality effort. Front-line employees and support staff, either together or separately, will need training on how to effectively carry out the library's customer service goals. This would typically be some form of client relations training involving work on listening, questioning, face-to-face communications, and relationship skills. Some employees may need training in new job skills as the result of changed work processes.

Managers and supervisors will need training in supporting front-line and support personnel in achieving customer service goals. Either as part of this training or separately, managers and supervisors may have to learn new human resource techniques for hiring employees, evaluating their work, and giving recognition, among other things.

CONCLUSION

Key activities that are important in implementing a TQM initiative, and the requisite skills and training requirements necessary at each step have been described. Neither this description nor the recommendations are intended to be all inclusive. While critical activities for a successful initiative have been delineated, there are many variations on the TQM theme.

There is little dispute among those experienced and knowledgeable in TQM that it is a change initiative, and it is being used or considered by organizations facing that challenge. As described in the introduction and extensively in the literature, the library community is facing its fair share of change.[12] From an individual, as well as institutional point of view, change is not something that comes easily. Many organizations prefer to deny or ignore it, and eventually go out of business. Some libraries are dealing with change and responding to the challenges of remaining viable. Therese Baker describes an effort to insure that off-campus students have access to library materials, including a toll-free 800 number to order articles and books.[13] The Baltimore County Public Library has developed a program to improve interpersonal skills in the reference interview called STAR (System Training for Accurate Reference).[14] Harvard's Kennedy School of Government library has established a suggestion book to record patron complaints.[15]

These are a few of the examples of library efforts to be responsive to patrons. Unfortunately, all too often, these efforts are simply piecemeal and not necessarily tied to other processes having an impact on organization performance; at times they may even work at cross purposes to other initiatives. A strength of the TQM approach is that is it designed to promote improvement as part of a comprehensive integrated (systems) approach.

Schlichter and Pemberton[16] report some less successful efforts to be responsive to patron needs. For example, a study of 122 public libraries in California showed that 94% of them had not carried out an evaluation in the last three years. Among those libraries that had conducted surveys, 78% had failed to initiate action in response to survey results. The authors speculate on a number of reasons for low acceptance of evaluation data, including the difficulty of "translating the results of such studies into concrete management decisions."[17]

One of the desirable aspects of TQM is that the analytical tools are rather straightforward and have been successfully used by all types of employees including professionals, clerks, and automotive mechanics. One of the clichés among TQM consultants is that "you don't have to be a rocket scientist to use TQM tools." This is not to say that implementing a full TQM transformation is easy; it isn't. But TQM does provide a way to insure that all elements of the organization are working toward a common goal.

At the ALA midwinter meeting, Susan Barnard suggested that the customer is one of the elements of TQM least familiar in the library community, but potentially one of the most beneficial.[18] If this is accurate, we need to enhance knowledge and awareness of the customer dimension. TQM is a useful approach for pursuing this end.

NOTES

1. James E. Swiss, "Adapting Total Quality Management (TQM) to Government," *Public Administration Review,* July-August 1992.

2. Leigh Estabrook and Chris Horak, "Public vs. Professional Opinion on Libraries: The Great Divide?" *Library Journal,* April 1, 1992.

3. Susan B. Barnard, "A Draft Model for Adopting TQM in a Research Library," A Report at the 1992 ALA Midwinter Meeting, January 25, 1992, p.3

4. Kathy Rebello et al., "Your Digital Future," *Business Week,* September 7, 1992, p.61.

5. Barnard, op. cit.

6. Kenneth B. Johnston, "The Shadow Organization," A reference paper of Kaset International, 1991.

7. Ron Cox, "Integrating Your Total Quality and Customer Service Efforts," A reference paper of Kaset International, 1991.

8. Leonard Berry et al., "Five Imperatives for Improving Service Quality," *Sloan Management Review,* Summer 1990, p.30.

9. Ibid., p.29.

10. Robert Desatnick, *Managing to Keep the Customer,* San Francisco: Jossey-Bass, 1988.

11. George D. Wagenheim and John H. Reurink, "Customer Service in Public Administration," *Public Administration Review,* May-June 1991, p.269.

12. S. Michael Malinconico, "Information's Brave New World," *Library Journal,* May 1, 1992; Ilene F. Rockman, ed., "Reference Librarian of the Future," *Reference Services Review,* Number 1, 1991; Anne K. Beaubien, "Recruiting the Best and the Brightest," *College and Research Library News,* May 1992.

13. Therese D. Baker, "Request Forms for Extended Campus Library Services," *College and Research Library News,* April 1992, pp. 260-261.

14. Laura J. Isenstein, "Get Your Reference Staff on the STAR Track," *Library Journal,* April 15, 1992.

15. Donald Alschiller, "Read Any Good (Suggestion) Books Lately?" *College and Research Library News,* February 1992.

16. Doris J. Schlichter and J. Michael Pemberton, "The Emperor's New Clothes? Problems of User Survey as a Planning Tool in Academic Libraries," *College and Research Libraries,* May 1992, p.257.

17. Ibid., p.258.

18. Barnard, op. cit., p.3.

Problem Solving Teams in a Total Quality Management Environment

Constance F. Towler

HOW INDIVIDUALS SOLVE PROBLEMS

The concept of problem solving in organizations has been around ever since there have been organizations, because ever since there have been organizations there have been problems. (It goes with the territory.) Individuals, by nature, are problem solvers. Individuals, by nature, are also problem causers. As a culture we have been trained to solve problems quickly, to get the solution behind us and get on to the next task in a hurry; therefore, we have often rushed to the fastest solution. As a consequence, some of us spend too much of our time fighting fires which are often caused by hasty *partial* solutions. We are so accustomed to this practice that we believe it is part of our job.

THE THREE ASPECTS OF TEAM PROBLEM SOLVING

But think about another scenario–think about teams of individuals solving problems once and for all–think about that same prob-

Constance F. Towler is Program Director, Harvard Quality Process, Harvard University, Cambridge, MA.

[Haworth co-indexing entry note]: "Problem Solving Teams in a Total Quality Management Environment." Towler, Constance F. Co-published simultaneously in the *Journal of Library Administration,* (The Haworth Press, Inc.) Vol. 18, No. 1/2, 1993, pp. 97-112; and: *Integrating Total Quality Management in a Library Setting* (ed: Susan Jurow, and Susan B. Barnard), The Haworth Press, Inc., 1993, pp. 97-112. Multiple copies of this article/chapter may be purchased from The Haworth Document Delivery Center. Call 1-800-3-HAWORTH (1-800-342-9678) between 9:00 - 5:00 (EST) and ask for DOCUMENT DELIVERY CENTER.

lem never coming back again. In this scenario, we might have time to do some of those tasks that keep getting added to our overflowing plates.

The team approach to problem solving brings together a multiplicity of people in an organization to perform three separate functions:

1. the team members bring in all of the aspects of a given problem, or, at least, more than any individual could encompass;
2. while the team is coming up with the problem solution, each "fix" to the problem is made in relation to all other aspects of the problem, so that the solution the team comes up with is one they have agreed can work;
3. the team then takes its solution and implements it on a day-to-day basis, fine-tuning it and making modifications as necessary.

Employees in today's workforce are seeking a chance to participate and want a greater say in decisions that affect them on the job; they want to be recognized. Involving employees in solving the problems of an organization enhances the productivity of the organization and the morale of the employees. The team members who solve a problem in the meeting room are actually the ones who are going to take the agreed-upon solution into the workplace and make it *work*.

Solutions determined in this way are more effective for organizations. Employees find that by cooperating with one another in problem solving they help to create real and positive change and move the organization forward.

Now that we have discussed what is needed and how well it works, let us outline a team training process that will implement this method of solving problems.

PROBLEM SOLVING TEAMS

With team problem solving, employees at every level in an organization get more involved in the day-to-day operations of their organization. The team gathers data to get at the root causes of a problem, analyzes why the problem is occurring, and fixes the problem once and for all. The results of the team effort will be improved work processes and the improved quality of service which the organization delivers. And the individuals or groups who receive that service will be more satisfied.

How Teams Are Formed and Their Size

The team should include representatives of all parts of the organization affected by the problem. The members of the team should include a vertical slice of the organization: the manager and/or supervisor of the group, the individuals who actually perform the work of the process being studied, and/or those who are affected by the process.

The size of the team will depend on the project to be undertaken. An ideal team size is six or eight individuals. If the team needs to be larger for some reason, sub-teams may be formed. These sub-teams perform tasks that the overall team has agreed to and then report back to that team.

Teams can be formed in several ways:

- within a group,
- cross-functionally,
- cross-departmentally,
- to include the external customer or vendor.

The best way to form a team depends upon the problem to be solved.

Some Cautions in Forming Teams

- "Pick the low hanging fruit." When beginning problem-solving team activities, select problems in processes that are not too complex and where success is fairly certain. Since the team members are new to the process, this provides a positive start for the team activities.
- Train the team members. Do not assume that everyone on the team knows how to solve problems. Teach them some basic

tools and techniques to help in the analysis, implementation and evaluation.

- Include a member of management if possible. This makes decision-making and communication much easier.

Roles in Teams

The use of small groups requires several roles that can help team effectiveness. The roles are:

1. facilitator
2. scribe
3. timekeeper
4. secondary facilitators

Each of the roles is described in some detail below.

1. Facilitator

A facilitator is a person who helps a team free itself from internal obstacles or difficulties so that it may more efficiently and effectively pursue its objectives in a given situation. The facilitator does not evaluate or contribute ideas to the problem definition or solution. The facilitator is responsible for all pre-meeting and post-meeting logistics, helps the team build agendas, assigns a timekeeper and a scribe (if no one volunteers), suggests tools and techniques, assures that the team is not jumping to conclusions, leads the group in the search for diversity and consensus, and guides process checks throughout the team meetings. The facilitator is not a member of the problem-solving team and may be responsible for supporting several teams at any given time. The facilitator can serve as a role model, demonstrating for team members some of the skills required for their roles.

As teams get to know each other and become more comfortable with the problem-solving process, an outside facilitator may not be necessary. The manager or another member of the group may assume the facilitator role.

2. Scribe

The scribe is responsible for recording the group's ideas, decisions, and recommendations. The scribe is the "group's memory." This role should rotate among team members, but members willing to scribe who are good at it may do it more often than others.

The scribe usually works at a flipchart easel. As each flipchart page is filled, the scribe posts it so that group members can go back for review at any time. The scribe keeps a running record of meeting progress and sends out notes to team members before the next meeting. The notes of the meetings will be very helpful when the team is ready to document its work.

3. Timekeeper

Teams usually have about one and one-half hours a week for their problem-solving meetings. Although there may be some flexibility, teams usually have time constraints. To help teams manage their time effectively, most agree on a game plan of how long to spend on each of the activities on the agenda.

The timekeeper has responsibility for monitoring how long the group is taking to accomplish its agenda topics, and giving regular updates to make team members aware of how far along they are. The group may decide to reallocate its time as the task progresses. It may even decide not to complete the task within the time limit. These are team decisions, not the timekeeper's personal choice. This role should rotate among team members.

4. Secondary Facilitators

All team members are expected to be active participants in the meeting. Responsibilities of the group members as secondary facilitators include keeping the facilitator in a neutral role, making sure that ideas are recorded accurately, making procedural suggestions, overruling suggestions of the facilitator, stopping activities for a process check, and generally determining the course of the meeting. It is important that all team members recognize that they share the responsibility for the success of the team.

Time Commitments of Problem-Solving Teams

Problem-Solving Team Training runs for eighteen hours; of these, twelve hours is spent on the six steps of the problem-solving process. Problem-solving teams usually meet once a week for one and one-half to two hours each meeting. Depending on the problem, teams may meet from twelve to fourteen weeks before they have completed all six steps of the Problem-Solving Process.

It has often been said that this process takes time. That is true. But, if we used to take time to do over again what we repaired so hurriedly in the past, why do we not now have the time to fix it the right way? By teaching the tools and techniques of this problem-solving process, we are equipping our employees with what they need to fix problems so they should never occur again.

PROBLEM-SOLVING TEAM TRAINING

There are seven components of the Problem-Solving Team Training:

1. Introduction to Total Quality Management
2. Customer Satisfaction
3. Meeting Management
4. Parker Team Player Survey
5. Interactive Skills
6. Consensus Decision Making
7. Problem-Solving Process

Each session begins with a warm-up exercise. On the first day this involves asking all of the participants for their objectives for the training program. At the end of each session, participants are asked to evaluate that particular session. A written evaluation is requested at the end of the program.

1. Introduction to Total Quality Management

By using the pre-reading material, participants report on an interview with their managers or supervisors. A video on the global quality movement introduces participants to the key concepts of Total Quality Management. These concepts include the focus on internal and external customers, identifying customer requirements, total employee involvement, the use of teams, consensus decision-making, top management leadership, cross-department cooperation, continuous improvement, and the role of education and training. Application of quality concepts and practices at Harvard University are reported and quality management activities at Harvard as a whole are reviewed.

2. Customer Satisfaction

The importance of customer satisfaction as the goal of Total Quality Management is stressed. Participants have a chance to report on good and bad service they have received in response to the customer service video "Remember Me." Also, participants are asked to share stories of excellent service delivered by themselves, co-workers, or work units.

3. Meeting Management

Participants learn how to use a basic method of meeting management that suggests the four roles in meetings: facilitator, scribe, timekeeper, and secondary facilitators. This method is practiced throughout the Team Training so all members have experience in all roles.

4. Parker Team Player Survey

Each participant is asked to complete the Parker Team Player Survey. This survey helps to identify styles as a team player. The results lead to an assessment of individual current strengths and provides a basis for a plan for increasing effectiveness as a team player. Once individual team styles are identified, teams may develop a profile of team strengths and discuss strategies for increasing team effectiveness.

There are four styles identified in the Survey: Contributor, Collaborator, Communicator, and Challenger. A mix of styles is helpful for a team to be most effective.

5. Interactive Skills

Participants learn to recognize and to use good group-member skills through presentation and exercises. Participants then practice and receive feedback on use of the skills in small-group problem-solving meetings during the remainder of the Problem-Solving Team Training. Group-member skills include proposing, building, seeking and giving information, testing for understanding, summarizing, supporting, and disagreeing.

6. Consensus Decision-Making

The importance of consensus decision-making is stressed. Participants learn a basic definition of consensus, including the psychological state of those who disagree with a decision but who are willing to support it. The role of the manager or supervisor in the consensus decision-making process is explored and discussed. The connection between total employee involvement and consensus is made.

It is stressed that every team should develop a list of meeting ground rules like the one below. The meaning of each item on the list should be agreed to by all members of the group. Once the list is developed, it is posted in the meeting room. The facilitator and all group members have the responsibility to hold each other accountable for abiding by the ground rules. In Problem-Solving Team Training the participants develop a set of ground rules which they agree to follow for the duration of the training:

1. Active listening.
2. Punctual attendance.
3. No one-on-one or side meetings.
4. Respect for agenda.
5. Willingness to reach consensus.
6. Freedom to check process and groundrules.
7. Freedom to disagree.

8. Active participation.
9. Sharing responsibility for team's progress.
10. Uninterrupted meetings.
11. Basic courtesy.
12. Confidentiality.
13. Quorum.

7. The Problem-Solving Process

The goal of getting employees involved is to give people increased influence over their work, as well as improving work processes and the quality of services provided. One of the major routes to achieving employee involvement is the creation of problem-solving teams: groups of employees who meet on a regular basis to identify and solve work-related problems.

The success of group problem solving is enhanced if a systematic, common, problem-solving process is taught to all participants of employee involvement groups. This common process provides groups with a road map to follow, a common language of problem solving, and a set of tools and techniques, some of which are statistical in nature.

Problem-solving training is delivered to teams and work groups which include a manager or supervisor. When people who work together learn new skills together, it is usually easier to transfer those skills to their work environment.

It is important for teams to communicate with management throughout the problem-solving process. The simple practice of sending notes of meetings or developing a form which is sent at the conclusion of each step is usually adequate.

Techniques that participants learn include:

- tools for generating ideas and collecting information
  (brainstorming, checksheets, interviewing, and surveying)
- tools for reaching consensus
  (list reduction, criteria rating forms, and weighted voting)
- tools for analyzing and displaying data
  (cause and effect analysis, force field analysis, histograms, Pareto analysis, and pie charts)
- tools for planning action
  (flow charts and Gantt charts)

The problem-solving process is taught using an extensive case study in which participants, acting as problem-solving teams, have to analyze an example of inefficient service.

In Quality Problem-Solving Team Training participants are taught a six-step process. The steps of the process are displayed in Figure 1.

The problem-solving process is very flexible, with application to a wide variety of concerns. The process is very data intensive, in the training setting, the data is provided for the participants. It is stressed, however, that extensive data gathering is necessary in the day-to-day work situation, to solve problems so they will not recur.

FIGURE 1. Problem-Solving Process[1]

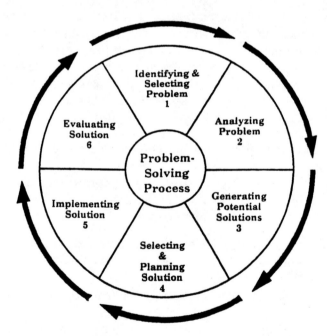

[1]Xerox Corporation, Leadership Through Quality, Problem-Solving Process User's Manual, 1986, p. i.

Following is a description of the steps in the Problem-Solving Process and the tools and techniques that participants learn.

Step 1. Identifying and Selecting a Problem

There are three tasks for the participants to achieve in this step:

1. identify the problem
2. review available data about the extent and nature of the problem
3. describe the problem in an "As-Is" statement and "Desired-State" statement

The participants are sorted into teams, six to eight members each. The teams are composed of individuals who are in the same work unit or individuals who will be working as a team to solve a problem after the training is completed. They are given background information on the extent and nature of the problem they are being asked to solve.

The team begins by brainstorming, a technique in which every team member identifies possible problems to address. These ideas are listed by the scribe. Each idea is discussed and the team reaches consensus on which problem to address. In making this decision, the team considers:

- time (do we have enough time to solve this problem?)
- resources (do we have enough resources to solve this problem?)
- importance (is this problem important enough for us to tackle?)
- need (is this where we should put our efforts?)

Once the problem has been identified, the team writes a problem statement (or "As-Is" statement). The problem statement is critical because the team will refer to it throughout the process. The problem statement should describe the situation as it currently exists and should include as much measurement as is available at the time. (Keep in mind that since this is a flexible process, the problem statement may be revised as the team progresses.)

Then the team writes a statement which describes their "Desired State," which is the result they will achieve when they have solved their problem. Each time the teams meet, they appoint or volunteer for the roles of: facilitator, scribe, timekeeper and presenter.

Example: As-Is statement:
"Fifteen percent of the original cataloging records contain errors."
Example: Desired-State statement:
"Reduce errors in original cataloging records by 50%."

Step 2. Analyzing the Problem

The team next collects data about the problem and analyzes it, looking for answers to several questions:

- does the data show the problem is real?
- what are its causes?
- what forces are affecting the problem?
- how widespread is the problem?

At this point, the team learns about the use of the following tools to analyze and display their data:

- A Pareto chart. Pareto analysis is based on the idea that by separating the "vital few" from the "trivial many" we can set priorities that focus on major problems.
- A cause and effect diagram (otherwise known as a "fishbone" or an Ishikawa diagram). This is a systematic way of looking at effects and causes that contribute to those effects. Similar factors are grouped together for clarity. (See Figure 2.)
- Histograms and pie charts.

Each team now produces a "fishbone," citing potential causes and all of their potential effects, and presents it to the class. One technique in producing the fishbone is to ask the question "why" five times. Each "why" uncovers another layer of the problem. Instead of randomly trying to think of possible causes, the fishbone exercise gives structure to the search for causes.

Step 3. Generating Potential Solutions

The participants are given a package of data on possible causes. The teams will answer questions in search of the three key causes

FIGURE 2. Cause and Effect Diagram[2]

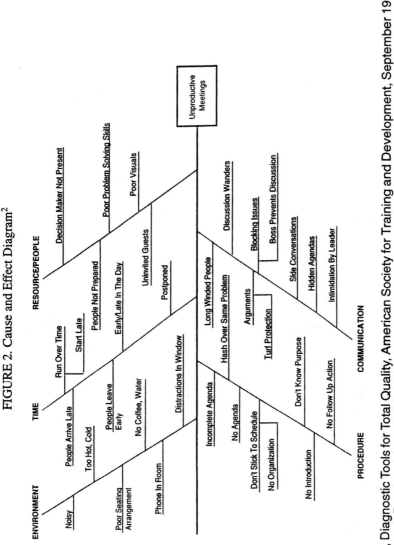

[2]INFO-LINE, Diagnostic Tools for Total Quality, American Society for Training and Development, September 1991, Issue 9109, p. 8 Reprinted from INFO-LINE. Copyright September 1991, American Society For Training And Development, Inc. Reprinted With Permission. All Rights Reserved.

for why the problem exists. The group then makes a list of possible solutions to their problem statement. Brainstorming is used to generate many solutions which are then defined, narrowed, and categorized into a manageable number of five or six solution sets. If items on the list are good ideas but not solutions that will directly help to achieve our current "Desired State," they are bracketed; they can then be considered at a future time.

The group is now introduced to the Criteria Rating Form. The use of this form helps groups to reach a decision on the best solution to work on from the list of five or six solutions. Each team produces a Criteria Rating Form and presents it to the class.

Throughout these steps of the problem-solving process, participants are reminded of the appropriate use of Interactive Skills and asked to think about what kind of group interactions will result in a successful session overall.

Step 4. Selecting and Planning a Solution

The teams now have one solution to their problem and they are ready to plan its implementation. They create a plan to bring about changes, a time frame for each step, and measurement criteria to monitor the solution. The plan includes breaking down what is to be done into manageable steps, assigning tasks and setting milestones, identifying a method of tracking the progress of the implementation, strategies for gaining commitment, contingency plans, and a way to evaluate how well the solution is working. The teams are introduced to the following action planning tools: PERT chart, flowchart, and Gantt chart. Each team is asked to develop a Gantt chart and an implementation plan.

Step 5. Implementing the Solution

The primary difference in this problem-solving process and the traditional "committee" or "task force" problem-solving approach of the past, is that the team will actually implement and evaluate the solution they have planned. They will not hand their solution over to management or any other group for this process to take place. This gives the team a responsibility they probably have not experienced before, and the facilitator should work particularly closely with the team through Steps 5 and 6.

The team carries out its plan in Step 5. If the plan needs modification, which is not unusual in the "real world" outside the conference room, the team makes those modifications.

Step 6. Evaluating the Solution

The team collects data on its results and compares it with the "Desired State Statement" from Step 1 to determine if they have met their goal. If not, they may need to begin the process over again or go back to a previous step. The team should also be on the look-out for what new problems might be created by solving this problem. Even if the goal has been met, the team will want to continue to monitor the solution to make sure that the situation continues to work, and that there are no new problems created by the solution itself.

Training Conclusion

The training is concluded with a review of the Problem-Solving Process steps, a review of the key concepts of quality management with a focus on customer service and work processes, a videotape of Baldrige Award Winners, a written evaluation, and graduation exercises. A member of senior management is invited to convey support, encouragement and appreciation for the efforts of the participants. Certificates of completion are presented to each individual as they are released to the "real world" to put into practice what they have learned.

FOLLOW-ON BENEFITS

It is important to note a valuable secondary effect of this type of training program. Participants are building up a sensitivity to the evolutionary nature of problems. People with the training we have been discussing will not only be able to solve existing problems in a more systematic, efficient, and effective way, they will also be able to sense potential problems and see when it is possible to avoid them before they start to cause trouble.

ACKNOWLEDGMENTS

I would like to thank Douglas Renick, Senior Consultant for Human Resource Development in the Center for Training and Development at Harvard University. Douglas has worked with me in the development of the Harvard Quality Process training curriculum over the past couple of years. Without his expert assistance and dedication to employee participation and team development, we would not be nearly as advanced in TQM training as we find ourselves today. I would also like to thank the Xerox Corporation, and, in particular, Kim Mitchell-Jasmine, for their very generous assistance as we began the Harvard Quality Process two years ago.

SUGGESTED SOURCES

The following resources have been used in researching and developing the Harvard Quality Process curriculum.

Doyle, Michael and David Straus. *How To Make Meetings Work.* New York: Jove Books, Berkeley Publishing Group, 1982.

Xerox Corporation. *USMG Partnership, The Way We Work, USMG Quality Office,* 1989.

Xerox Corporation. Leadership Through Quality. *Problem-Solving Process User's Manual,* 1986.

Xerox Corporation. *New Employee Quality Training Participant Workbook,* 1986.

Tools for Measuring
and Improving Performance

Susan Jurow

"If you can't measure something, you can't understand it; if you can't understand it, you can't control it; if you can't control it, you can't improve it." [1]

Over the past thirty years, academic and research libraries have grown larger and more complex. Their financial fortunes have waxed and waned with the economy. When budgets grow tighter, accountability takes on a greater prominence. In looking for ways to argue for more funding, library administrators and managers have come to realize that much of the data they collect relates to inputs and outputs. It does not provide information about the degree to which the library is achieving desired results. This problem has led to increased efforts to find more meaningful performance measures.

This recognition of the need for better approaches to measuring library operations coincides with the growing interest in applying TQM methodologies to not-for-profit organizations. The timing could not be more propitious. Many service providers, including librarians, are nervous about quantifying their efforts. This is often based on previous experience with management consultants who

Susan Jurow is Director of the Association of Research Libraries' Office of Management Services, Washington, DC.

[Haworth co-indexing entry note]: "Tools for Measuring and Improving Performance." Jurow, Susan. Co-published simultaneously in the *Journal of Library Administration,* (The Haworth Press, Inc.) Vol. 18, No. 1/2, 1993, pp. 113-126; and: *Integrating Total Quality Management in a Library Setting* (ed: Susan Jurow, and Susan B. Barnard), The Haworth Press, Inc., 1993, pp. 113-126. Multiple copies of this article/chapter may be purchased from The Haworth Document Delivery Center. Call 1-800-3-HAWORTH (1-800-342-9678) between 9:00 - 5:00 (EST) and ask for DOCUMENT DELIVERY CENTER.

113

tried to reduce professional work to numbers and dollars, without understanding its complexities. TQM methodology provides an opportunity to support the development of library performance measures that focus on how best to meet the needs of users.

A primary focus of Total Quality Management (TQM) is the continuous improvement of operations. To engage in an ongoing effort of this nature, data gathering and analysis processes must be in place that provide meaningful information to managers, administrators, and those actually engaged in doing the work. It also requires an approach to measurement that leads to problem solving, not an evaluative process that apportions reward and blame. When this concept is added to another TQM premise, that the operational process is more often to blame for problems than individual workers, a powerful tool exists for enlisting staff support for any improvement effort.

MEASUREMENT AND IMPROVEMENT

Past Practice

Dr. W. Edwards Deming, the acknowledged "godfather" of TQM, has articulated fourteen points that he considers the core of the TQM philosophy. Two of them relate specifically to measurement. Point three is "cease dependence on mass inspection," and point number twelve is "eliminate numerical quotas." These two points are directed at the way supervisors have traditionally built measurable accountability into their systems; by setting goals and reviewing the work performed by others.

What a supervisor measures with these approaches is the degree to which an individual is working in relation to expectations that have been set. What is not measured is how well the individual is capable of performing or whether the desired results are being accomplished.

Counting and/or inspecting everything that is done implies that defects are expected to occur. Finding a problem or mistake at the end of a process doesn't improve the quality of the product. It simply creates a situation where rework is required. Goal setting establishes arbitrary limits on what can or should be accomplished. Goals are often based on averages that some can't meet and others are capable of exceeding.

TQM Approach

Improvement implies an understanding of the current situation and the projection of a desired result that is both different and better. Because TQM approaches improvement as a continuous process, progress is what is measured, not just arrival at an end state. Philip Crosby, one of the TQM "gurus" has written, "Measurement is just the habit of seeing how we're going along."[2] If it is not possible to measure the critical elements in the current situation, then it is difficult to discern the degree to which they have moved toward a desired state, or if, in fact, they have arrived.

Many experienced workers feel they have developed an intuitive sense regarding their performance, but anecdotal evidence does not allow improvement to be understood with any degree of accuracy. There are other reasons to employ effective measurement practices in the workplace. Data instills confidence. It is difficult to argue with numbers, and the results of data-gathering efforts often facilitate changes that may have been blocked previously by entrenched perspectives.

Data collection can also be used to focus organizational attention on relevant issues. The decision to measure a particular effort should be driven by the importance of the activity and not just how easy it is to count. The feasibility of a particular improvement effort is also established in the process of determining the appropriate measures for the targeted activity.

The measurement of effort also leads to acknowledgment of results, and recognition of achievements can be a powerful motivation tool. Involving the staff who are doing the work in the process of determining what to assess and how to measure it increases their sense of ownership and pride in accomplishment. It also increases the likelihood that there will be a commitment to undertake the changes indicated by the process. Once staff begin to see measurement as a tool to better understand the impact of their efforts, rather than as a punitive evaluation tool, TQM becomes a powerful tool for developing a learning climate in the organization.

SYSTEMATIC APPROACH

A fundamental concept in the TQM approach is the systematic review of operational processes. The goal is to develop an understanding of the root causes of problems, so that the processes can be improved. These processes are often complex, and the root cause of the problem difficult to uncover. Through the collection and analysis of data by the people who do the work, the organization stands the best chance of developing new approaches that have the greatest likelihood for long-term success.

When work processes are examined, it is often found that the complexity in the system is the result of an overlay of "fixes." For a variety of reasons, organizations often attempt to solve a problem in the middle of a process without rethinking the entire process. It may be because the system is trying to work around an individual. Sometimes it is because the perception exists that resources are not available to provide a comprehensive resolution. It is also possible that no one perceives that the process as a whole is flawed. Each "fix" has the potential for unforeseen consequences that can lead to new problems. In the end, a process can become so complicated that it is difficult to discern the root cause of a problem.

The purpose of an operational review is not to solve problems per se, but to seek ways of improving the process to better accomplish the work. There are four things to be alert for in the review: mistakes and/or defects, breakdown and/or delays, inefficiencies, and variations.[3] Many organizations have procedures in place to fix mistakes after they happen. When mistakes are expected, these procedures are needed to compensate for them. For example, the need for a review process after books have been received on an approval plan indicates an expectation that the plan will not be able to predict the correct titles accurately enough.

Breakdowns and delays do not harm products, but they are particularly bad in the context of a service operation. A photocopy machine that breaks down regularly causes a significant inconvenience to the patron and takes staff away from other work. In an interlibrary loan operation, it can be disastrous. A set of forms may have been designed to comply with the regulations of the host institution, e.g., the university or the city; the library may go on using the forms long after the regulations have changed or disappeared because no one remembers the reason for their existence. Variation forces staff to add steps to standard processes. The larger the variety of borrowing privileges a library offers, the greater the number of special approaches the circulation staff must take.

Many people are uncomfortable with mathematical concepts, and the idea of having to learn and use statistical measures can be daunting. One contribution TQM has made to the practice of management is to popularize several simple, but effective management and planning tools. The graphic products of these tools make them easily accessible to those who are uncomfortable trying to interpret numbers in columns and tables.

The Tool Kit

Throughout the TQM literature, reference is made to graphical planning, action and control tools. These techniques support the systematic approach to understanding and measuring internal performance gaps. There are several excellent books that provide clear examples on how to apply them.[4] There are five tools that represent different stages of a TQM inquiry that will be covered here. They show how simple, but powerful these techniques can be.

The Shewhart Cycle

The Shewhart Cycle, also known as PDCA (Plan-Do-Check-Act), provides a simple way of presenting the series of activities that make up a process improvement project. During the Planning stage, problems are identified, and the problem to be studied is selected. In stage two, Doing, the problem is analyzed, and the root cause is determined. Possible solutions are also identified and selected at this stage. The solution is tested during the Checking stage. Implementation and evaluation of the solution takes place during the Acting stage. As shown in Figure 1, four tools are used at different stages of the Shewhart Cycle.

Flowcharts

The flowchart is the most fundamental of tools because it allows staff to represent graphically all the steps in the process being examined. It is often an eye-opening exercise, and frequently, immediate changes in procedure result from the revelations at this

FIGURE 1

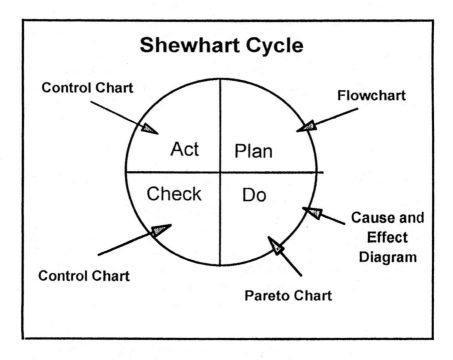

stage. An important consideration in using this technique is the level of detail required. This technique is designed to illuminate, not to overwhelm the investigators with details and minutiae that paralyze the inquiry (Figure 2).

Cause-and-Effect Diagrams

Also known as the "fishbone diagram" or "Ishikawa diagram," this technique is an effective way of clarifying possible causes of a particular problem. It depicts the factors discovered through the work flow analysis in a graphical form. It is useful because it organizes the factors, so that their relationship to each other is as clear as their relationship to the problem itself. The outcome of the exercise remains in focus because the problem is displayed at one end of the diagram (Figure 3).

FIGURE 2

Flow Chart

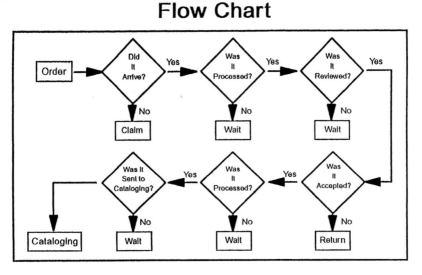

Tracking the Acquisitions Process

Pareto Charts

While exploring a process, investigators are likely to turn up many different problems that contribute to mistakes, delays, inefficiencies and variation. Pareto charts illustrate the degree to which each factor contributes to the overall problem. They often support the 80/20 principle articulated by the early nineteenth century economist, Vilfredo Pareto. It holds that eighty percent of trouble comes from twenty percent of the problems (Figure 4).

Control Charts

After quantifiable data has been collected, there are a number of statistical tools for refining the nature and extent of a problem. Control charts highlight variation in a system. They help the investigators to assess the relative importance of deviations from the

FIGURE 3

Cause and Effect Diagram

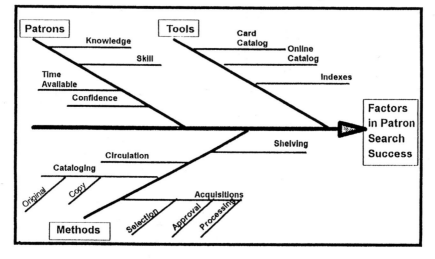

norm and in discovering whether the variations are cyclical or sporadic in nature. With this information, it is much easier to pinpoint causes. Once the data has been gathered and analyzed, it can also be used to set expectations about the level of activity in that area (Figure 5).

Benchmarking

Benchmark: "a: A point of reference from which measurements can be made; b: something that serves as a standard by which others may be measured."[5]

The term "benchmarking" has become identified with a key process used in TQM efforts. It represents a structured, proactive change effort designed to help achieve high performance through comparative assessment. It is a process that establishes an external standard to which internal operations can be compared. Benchmarking provides an opportunity for new thinking about what are realistic or feasible targets. It does this by contributing information about what other organizations are able to accomplish in the same or similar operations.

FIGURE 4

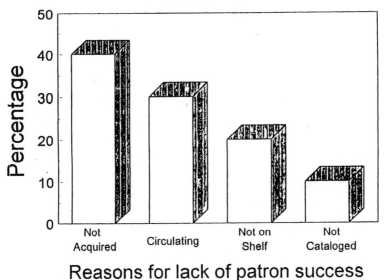

Pareto Chart

Reasons for lack of patron success

Traditionally, organizations have set goals based on internal information. Goal setting focuses primarily on defining the desired end state to be achieved. It reflects generally expected or desired change in local past practice. The difference between benchmarking and goal setting is also a question of focus. Benchmarking focuses as much on the means, or how to achieve the target, as it does on the projected end state.

Benchmarking seems like a logical approach to improving operations, but there are a number of psychological hurdles that may need to be overcome before it is accepted. "Copy cat" is one of those epithets children learn in childhood. It reflects the greater emphasis in American culture on personal achievement, rather than on team work or "adaptive creativity" that focuses on improvement. There is also the sense of pride (that can slip into arrogance) over the superiority of what has been developed locally. Outside

FIGURE 5

Control Chart

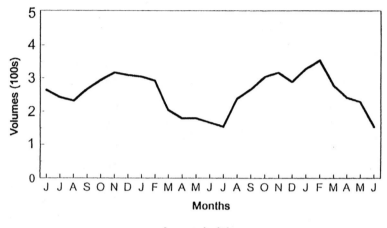

Acquisitions

ideas are often criticized because they are different from the current approach, not because they have been weighed on their merits.

The TQM literature specifies several types of benchmarking; two of these would be particularly useful for initial efforts within the library community. The first is called competitive or performance benchmarking. It examines the performance of exemplars in the same field or industry. In libraries, this could mean examining cataloging or circulation in another library, or examining online search services in an information delivery company.

The second type is called functional or process benchmarking. It seeks and studies the best practitioners of a particular function, no matter what the type of business. In this case, a library might examine the way banks organize and handle transactions at the teller windows, as a way of rethinking the process of handling transactions at the reference desk. Barcoding began as an inventory control device in grocery stores. Library use of this technique is an example of the migration of effective strategies across industry boundaries.

Over the past five years, the TQM literature has exploded with books and articles on benchmarking. Some deal with why to do it, others with how to do it, and still others with how we did it. GOAL/ QPC, a not-for-profit organization that supports dissemination of information on TQM, and Gregory Watson, author of *The Benchmarking Workbook*, use a model, illustrated in Figure 6, that could be easily adapted to the library environment.

In the initial planning stage, the organization reexamines its activities to identify critical processes, and knowledge of its customers is reviewed. Flowcharts are prepared for internal operations, and gaps between customer needs and the ability of the operation to meet those needs are identified. In the research stage, criteria are established to evaluate the information collected, and metrics are developed to measure the relevant processes. While the collection of quantifiable data is important, the focus of the inquiry should be primarily on the methods and practices used by the organization being studied.

Observation is the third stage. Training will be needed for those designated to gather the information, and forms should be developed to ensure consistency and comparability. The compilation of the data is considered part of this stage. The analysis stage, stage

FIGURE 6

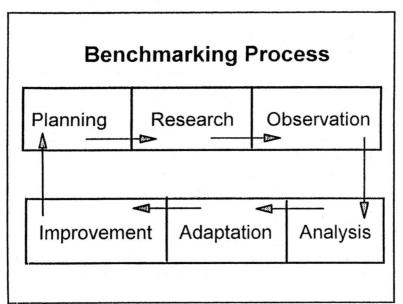

four, focuses on applying the lessons learned from the experience to current practices. Gaps between the local performance and that of the organization being studied are located and calibrated. New approaches are outlined.

The last two stages, adaptation and improvement, deal with the integration of new approaches into operations. Communication is a key to success at this point in the process. Changes seldom come easily, and requests for change in operating procedures are often viewed as implied criticism about the way things have been done in the past. It is helpful if findings can be put into the context of broad principles before being implemented more narrowly as applications. Stage six, improvement, closes the loop, and sets the cycle in motion again. It is appropriate at this time to examine the full process to see how it might be improved for the next benchmarking project.

One key to a successful benchmarking project is the development of partnerships. Winners of the Malcolm Baldrige National Quality Award are required to open their doors to others, so that their practices may be studied. Not everyone wants to take the time or expend the effort required to share their approaches with others. In their article in this volume, "Creating Partnerships: Forging a Chain of Service Quality," Richard Lynch, Lois Bacon and Ted Barnes suggest ways in which libraries can develop partnerships with their vendors to improve the quality of services delivered to library patrons.

There are ways that a benchmarking effort can lead to less than successful outcomes. The choice of practices to be benchmarked is critical. It is a waste of precious resources to put effort into assessments that do not directly contribute to improving the quality of a particular process or to customer satisfaction. Another pitfall is not allowing sufficient time for the study, analysis and design. Understanding a process, so that it can be adapted to local conditions, requires considerable staff resources.

Although it is time-consuming, benchmarking is a practice which has multiple benefits. It is an operational improvement tool, and it also plays an important role in the development of a learning culture. It not only helps an organization better understand how to operate efficiently and effectively, it provides a methodology for constant examination and renewal. In the process, staff learn how to gather and analyze data and how to work in teams. Because the benchmarking process is generally undertaken by those engaged in the work, it also builds a profound commitment to make the proposed changes work.

CONCLUSION

One of the criticisms often heard about TQM is that it is just another management fad. Over the last fifty years, managers and staff alike have had to learn techniques and processes purported to improve productivity and/or the products of their labor, only to have those practices debunked and displaced by the next round of approaches. Another way of looking at this history is to identify the ways in which each new set of concepts developed from the previous one, building on its strengths, and testing alternatives to compensate for its weaknesses.

If TQM fades as a management tool at some point in the future, it will have left behind its own important legacy in two key concepts. The first is the need to focus on the customer in the development of products and the delivery of services. The second is the need to be constantly aware of process both in development and delivery, and vigilant for opportunities for improvement. Data collection and measurement are simply means and tools, but they represent a new set of assumptions and a different attitude toward the delivery of library services.

A question that is often asked is, "Is it worth it to take all this time and effort to measure things, especially if we're pretty sure we know the answer?" Philip Crosby says that the "price of conformance is what is necessary to spend to make things come out right."[6] He includes both process and product, as well as efforts at preventing problems and checking for problems. The response may be another question, "How much do you care if you get it right?"

NOTES

1. H.J. Harrington. *The Improvement Process.* (New York: McGraw-Hill, 1987), p.103.

2. P. Crosby. *Quality Without Tears.* (New York: McGraw-Hill, 1984), p.108.

3. P.R. Scholtes. *The Team Handbook: How to Use Teams to Improve Quality.* (Madison, WI: Joiner Associates, 1988), p.2-11.

4. I recommend three books: Moran, J.W., R.P. Talbot and R.M. Benson. *A Guide to Graphical Problem-Solving Processes*. Milwaukee, WI: ASQC Quality Press, 1990; Brassard, M. *The Memory Jogger Plus+*. Methuen, MA: GOAL/ QPC, 1989; and Scholtes, P.R. *The Team Handbook: How to Use Teams to Improve Quality*. Madison, WI: Joiner Associates, 1988.

5. *Webster's Ninth New Collegiate Dictionary*. (Springfield, MA: Merriam-Webster, 1984), p.143.

6. Crosby, p.86.

SUPPORTING TOTAL QUALITY MANAGEMENT EFFORTS

Quality Reward and Awards: Quality Has Its Own Reward, but an Award Helps Speed the Process

W. David Penniman

INTRODUCTION

This article is not about a technique for fixing minor problems in our libraries. It is about a means for radically revising the way we do business (even though many don't like to think of a library in that sense). But why should we want radical change when our libraries have a fine history of contribution to this nation? It is true

W. David Penniman is President of the Council on Library Resources, Washington, DC.

[Haworth co-indexing entry note]: "Quality Reward and Awards: Quality Has Its Own Reward, but an Award Helps Speed the Process." Penniman, David W. Co-published simultaneously in the *Journal of Library Administration,* (The Haworth Press, Inc.) Vol. 18, No. 1/2, 1993, pp. 127-136; and: *Integrating Total Quality Management in a Library Setting* (ed: Susan Jurow, and Susan B. Barnard), The Haworth Press, Inc., 1993, pp. 127-136. Multiple copies of this article/ chapter may be purchased from The Haworth Document Delivery Center. Call 1-800-3-HAWORTH (1-800-342-9678) between 9:00 - 5:00 (EST) and ask for DOCUMENT DELIVERY CENTER.

127

that our libraries, be they academic, public, school or special, have made major contributions to our form of democratic society. The demand for information about Western forms of library operations and technology by newly unfettered Eastern European countries is evidence, if more were needed, of the success our libraries have experienced to date. But in the United States, as in these Eastern countries, the times are changing. Our economic conditions dictate more than traditional "belt-tightening."

We could choose (or have chosen for us) a financially-driven operating model that is developed by others who have budgetary responsibility for the institutions in which our libraries reside. In some cases, it already feels like that has happened. Complaints that the "bean counters" have taken over are usually shorthand ways of saying that the bottom line has become the driving force in an organization. (Bottom line in a not-for-profit operation is typically the difference between revenue and expenses. If it is positive, it is labelled a "fund balance"; if it is negative, it is called a deficit and is often accompanied by draconian and short-sighted cost cutting measures.) But given current economic conditions and the lack of an alternative approach to holding down or cutting costs, who can blame the leaders of our institutions for embracing a purely financially-focused model? Without a viable alternative to meeting financial objectives, such a model seems most appealing–even though it may be short sighted.

The major problem with choosing the bottom line as a driving force is that it is not customer focused, and without customers an institution cannot long survive. Despite the reluctance of many librarians to consider their patrons as customers, there is a real value in looking at those whom libraries serve through this lens. Furthermore, I believe that it is far more fruitful to focus on customer requirements (the quality model) than cost cutting alone (the rigid financial model). By focusing on customer requirements, the library can preserve what has made it such a special institution: its service orientation. So, the model that best fits the library in this time of radical change is one built around the quality thrust, and such a model calls for systematic and quantitative measures of performance.

MEASUREMENT VERSUS STANDARDS

Daniel Seymour, in his book on causing quality in higher education,[1] makes the point that quality *is* measurement. He draws a distinction, however, between externally imposed standards and internal measures that are derived from customer need. Accrediting processes are generally based on external standards and measure conformance to those standards.[2] Such a conformance approach is also preached by Philip Crosby in his writings (e.g., *Quality Without Tears*).[3] Failure to meet conformance standards places an institution in a "worst case" category and may deny it the right to serve its customers.

Of more use to institutions seeking to change would be an evaluation procedure that rewards a commitment to improvement on a continuing basis, not a pat on the back for being "OK" at the time of review. Some examples of "best cases" would also be helpful.

Seymour, in discussing the standards established for college libraries by the Association of College and Research Libraries, writes:

> Conformance to standards, therefore, may be a necessary but certainly not a sufficient condition for quality in libraries. The internal customer is less interested in standards and formulas than they (sic) are in a user-based definition of quality–"fitness for use."[4] (p. 53)

It is this concept of fitness for use (i.e., meeting customer needs and expectations) that makes the establishment of new measures of quality in libraries so compelling. By establishing procedures that focus on processes and the customer and that emphasize continual improvement rather than the achievement of an acceptable state of being (accreditation), libraries of all types can benefit from each other's experiences. Continual improvement processes are not specific to one type of library. Therefore, mechanisms for exchange of information among very different types of libraries are needed in order to reap the best from lessons learned. That is what leads me to propose an award for library quality tailored after the Malcolm Baldrige Award used in the commercial sector.

THE BALDRIGE AWARD

The award is named after Malcolm Baldrige, who served as Secretary of Commerce from 1981 until his accidental death in 1987, and was created by Public Law 100-107 in 1987. The intent of the award is to help improve quality and productivity in U.S. companies by:

- creating a pride of recognition while increasing profits
- providing examples to others of effective quality programs
- establishing guidelines by which organizations can evaluate their own quality programs
- providing sufficient detailed information on how winning organizations were able to change their cultures so that others interested in doing the same can follow suit

A detailed description of the 1992 award categories and criteria is available from the National Institute of Standards and Technology,[5] responsible for managing the award. Highlights of the categories evaluated are presented in Table 1 to provide a sense of the scope and focus of the program. Since its inception in 1987 (first awards were made in 1988), the program has gone through its own "process improvement." The latest criteria reflects a reduction in the number of items evaluated and a shift in point scores to add weight to the results achieved in customer satisfaction. In addition, the introductory material contained on the form has been expanded to add value as a training and design tool, as well as to serve as the award application.

A brief review of the categories/items indicates that the award is based on a detailed and rigorous evaluation of a wide array of factors that all go into a total quality perspective. Details about each category are included in the award application guidelines. It is instructive, in addition, to review the range of scores and those characteristics that would be expected of an applicant falling within each range. The scoring criteria are summarized in Table 2.

Clearly, an organization cannot hope to achieve the highest score without a total commitment to a quality philosophy of the type

TABLE 1
1992 Examination Categories/Items with Relative Weights [7]

Categories/Items	Percent of Total
Leadership	9
Senior Executive Leadership	
Management for Quality	
Public Responsibility	
Information and Analysis	8
Scope and Management of Quality and Performance Data and Information	
Competitive Comparisons and Benchmarks	
Analysis and Uses of Organization-Level Data	
Strategic Quality Planning	6
Strategic Quality and Organization Performance Planning Process	
Quality and Performance Plans	
Human Resources Development and Management	15
Human Resource Management	
Employee Involvement	
Employee Education and Training	
Employee Performance and Recognition	
Employee Well-Being and Morale	
Management of Process Quality	14
Design and Introduction of Quality Products and Services	
Process Management -- Product and Service Production and Delivery Processes	
Process Management -- Business Processes and Support Services	
Supplier Quality	
Quality Assessment	
Quality and Operational Results	18
Product and Service Quality Results	
Organization Operational Results	
Business Process and Support Service Results	
Supplier Quality Results	
Customer Focus and Satisfaction	30
Customer Relationship Management	
Commitment to Customers	
Customer Satisfaction Determination	
Customer Satisfaction Results	
Customer Satisfaction Comparisons	
Future Requirements and Expectations of Customers	
Total	100

TABLE 2

Scoring Criteria

Score	Evidence
0%	anecdotal approach with no system evident
10 - 40%	beginnings of systematic prevention approach in some major areas of operation with some positive trends
50%	sound, systematic approach with some evidence of integration. Applied in most major areas and some support areas. Positive trends in most major areas and some evidence that results are linked to approach
60 - 90%	sound, systematic approach with integration and evidence of refinement cycles. Applied in major areas and some to many support areas with good to excellent results in major areas and positive trends in some to many support areas. Evidence of causal links.
100%	sound, systematic prevention basis refined through cyclic improvement process and with excellent integration. Deployed through all major and support areas in all operations with world-class results in major areas and good to excellent results in support areas. Results are sustained and causal link is clear.
	(Note: Prevention in this context means prevention of problems or failures to meet quality standards.)

described in some of the references listed at the end of this article as well as works mentioned in other articles in this issue.[6]

REWARDS OF AN AWARD SYSTEM

There are at least eight benefits or rewards to be gained from implementing a quality award within the library community. These are not listed in priority order (except that the last is the *most* important):

Trained Evaluators

In order to adequately judge the applicants for such an award, it would be necessary to certify a fairly large number of individuals who were skilled at evaluating applications (just as the Baldrige award does). These individuals would become the critical mass of "quality experts" within our profession, able to help and consult with libraries as well as to serve as judges for the award.

Specific Objectives

An award with detailed categories and criteria patterned after the Baldrige award would help to specify clear objectives for those organizations/leaders who want to begin the route to improved quality. While cost cutting may still be necessary, each cut must be evaluated against the test of "customer focus." Study of the Baldrige criteria is a detailed lesson in how to begin to achieve the goal of comprehensive quality in the corporate world. A similar set of criteria is needed for the environments in which non-corporate libraries operate.

Documentation of Organization's Efforts

In order for an organization to apply for the award, it would need to document its efforts in the quality area. This would not only benefit the applying library, but would also serve to inform other parts of the organization (and senior leadership) who might not be aware of the quality efforts under way within the library.

Validation of Current Quality Programs in Libraries

For those libraries already well under way in a quality program, the application for such an award (to say nothing of winning an award) would validate their efforts.

Examples of "Best Practices" (Winners of Award)

Should a library win the award, it would become an example of the application of "best practices" within a particular area. Because winners must share their methods (a requirement of the award), these best practices would begin to migrate throughout the library community. Note that it is important for such migration to occur across library types as well.

Open Door for Others Wanting to Learn

The "open-door" requirement for winning organizations represents a major commitment to help other organizations eager to learn. This commitment would provide a stronger sense of leadership among the libraries that have worked through some of the tough issues of becoming quality organizations.

Wider Publicity About Libraries

An award properly managed and publicized would bring prestige and recognition to the library community in a form and area understood by other leaders in this nation and beyond. Quality is becoming a universal "language."

Better Service for Customers

The ultimate payoff of any quality effort is improved service for customers. Meeting or exceeding their expectations consistently is what makes a world-class organization, and that cannot be achieved without a total commitment to quality. A quality award program would help show the way to that goal.

PROPOSED ACTION PLAN

There are several steps that need to be taken to create a quality award of the type described here. I believe the library community should start now to take the steps listed below. I believe that there are several organizations representing various segments of the library community that are ready and willing to help undertake the tasks required, including the Council on Library Resources.

- Identify award sponsor
  (includes provision of appropriate trophy/plaque)
- Select award administrator
  (responsible for managing the overall process)
- Adapt Baldrige award criteria
  and application form
  (work with NIST to apply outside the corporate environment)
- Publicize award
  (announce availability of award throughout library community)
- Train evaluators
  (use Baldrige process for this initially)
- Encourage applications for award
  (set goal of 1994 for first applicants)

CONCLUSION

The time has never been better for the library community to introduce such an award. Many libraries are now investigating total quality management programs, and parent institutions are also looking toward such programs. The award program would help focus energy on a process that can help institutions now experiencing significant pressure to change. The path has already been blazed in the corporate environment and most of the work on detailing such an award has already been done. It is now up to the library community to take up the challenge and pursue its own quality award–and rewards.

NOTES

1. Daniel T. Seymour. *On Q: Causing Quality in Higher Education.* New York: Macmillan, 1992.

2. Mimi Harris Steadman and Ralph A. Wolff "Evaluating Library Quality in the Accreditation Process: What Changes Do New Technologies Bring?" Discussion paper prepared for the Accrediting Commission for Senior Colleges and Universities, November 21, 1991.

3. Philip B. Crosby. *Quality Without Tears.* New York: New American Library, 1984.

4. Seymour.

5. National Institute of Standards and Technology. *1992 Award Criteria, Malcolm Baldrige National Quality Award.* Gaithersburg, Md.: no date. (*Application Forms and Instructions* are also available from the same source for individual copy orders only.)

6. Kaoru Ishikawa. Translated by David J. Ju. *What is Total Quality Control? The Japanese Way.* Englewood Cliffs, N.J.: Prentice Hall, 1985, and Shigeru Mizuno. *Company-Wide Total Quality Control.* Tokyo, Japan: Asian Productivity Organization, 1988.

7. National Institute of Standards and Technology. p. 12.

Creating Partnerships:
Forging a Chain of Service Quality

Richard Lynch
Lois Bacon
Ted Barnes

The future belongs to those who prepare for it.

−Anonymous

Results are obtained by exploiting opportunities, not by solving problems.

−Peter Drucker

INTRODUCTION

Librarians in one form or another have always helped people find information, understand how it is organized, and master the various tools to get at it. While the basic mission of the librarian may appear the same, dramatic new blueprints and partnerships are emerging to accomplish these tasks:

Richard Lynch is Quality Manager for The Faxon Company in Westwood, MA. Lois Bacon and Ted Barnes are Quality and Process Innovation Consultants at The Faxon Company.

[Haworth co-indexing entry note]: "Creating Partnerships: Forging a Chain of Service Quality." Lynch, Richard, Lois Bacon, and Ted Barnes. Co-published simultaneously in the *Journal of Library Administration,* (The Haworth Press, Inc.) Vol. 18, No. 1/2, 1993, pp. 137-155; and: *Integrating Total Quality Management in a Library Setting* (ed: Susan Jurow, and Susan B. Barnard), The Haworth Press, Inc., 1993, pp. 137-155. Multiple copies of this article/chapter may be purchased from The Haworth Document Delivery Center. Call 1-800-3-HAWORTH (1-800-342-9678) between 9:00 - 5:00 (EST) and ask for DOCUMENT DELIVERY CENTER.

137

- *The research libraries of the Washington D.C. area have formed a partnership to strengthen interlibrary cooperation. They have developed a common online system, established a delivery system to expedite interlibrary loans, and share an off site storage facility.[1] The partnership provides better access to more materials and provides faster delivery cycle times for interlibrary loans.*
- *Libraries are linking up with The Faxon Company for Table of Contents and article information. In turn, Faxon is working with publishers to handle copyright clearance for document delivery directly to library patrons. Articles are received "just-in-time" for specific research needs.*
- *At the University of Houston Libraries, an expert system called "Reference Expert" provides users with an alternative to asking questions at the reference desk. Not only can help be provided twenty-four hours a day, but this resource is one of the choices on public computers.[2]*
- *At the University of California-Los Angeles business school, plans are in the works to combine the library and computing functions (i.e., the storage of knowledge and the means of processing it). Library and computing services will not only occupy the same facility, but will become intermingled as a true information resource center.[3]*
- *The High Performance Computing Act (1992) includes the formation of the National Research Education Network (NREN) which links research and educational institutions, government, and industry to ensure access to high performance computing systems, electronic information resources, and other research facilities. Libraries function in this partnership as resources for information and provide access to the data on the network.[4]*

Given the rapid technological advancements in networks, PCs and CD-ROMs, and trends in the "economics" of information, new *partnerships* must be identified, nurtured and sustained. Libraries have many possible partners from which to chose: authors, end users, departments within the university/institution, other libraries, associations, publishers, agents, and software and hardware vendors. But how are these partnerships initiated? Which ones are most important? And how are ideas and blueprints turned into operating realities?

THE CHALLENGE

The challenge facing today's librarian is similar to the hurdle facing manufacturers and other service providers–do more with less. The explosion of material, the means of accessing that material, and the cost of material are staggering. Research based on data from The Faxon Company's database of serial titles, shows that in 1978, there were 65,000 orderable serial and periodical publications, and in 1991, there were 109,204–a 68% increase. The greatest area of growth during that period was in the science and technology category which experienced a 427% jump. The yearly, domestic rate for all orderable journals in the Faxon title database also rose dramatically, from an average of $40 per year in 1978 to $168 in 1991. At the same time, library budgets have not kept pace with this growth. Of the eighty member libraries which responded to a survey by the Association of Research Libraries in 1991, over half faced budget cuts in 1991 and a little over 60% reported they expected budget cuts again in 1992.[5]

Increasingly, librarians, like all other information providers, are turning to technology to create new opportunities and partnerships for service identification and more cost-effective service delivery. Implicit in this new partnership is a new role for the librarian and information provider as highlighted in Figure 1.

For many librarians, the transition to information catalyst is well underway and new positions such as "system librarian" and "computer-based services librarian" are emerging to provide a wide range of electronic services. During this transition, strong partners can help to create new possibilities. But in practice, partnerships can be complex and transient. And the benefits of partnerships are not without costs, as described below.

BENEFITS OF PARTNERSHIPS

Partnerships are flourishing in industries ranging from automobile manufacturing to travel agencies to education. For example,

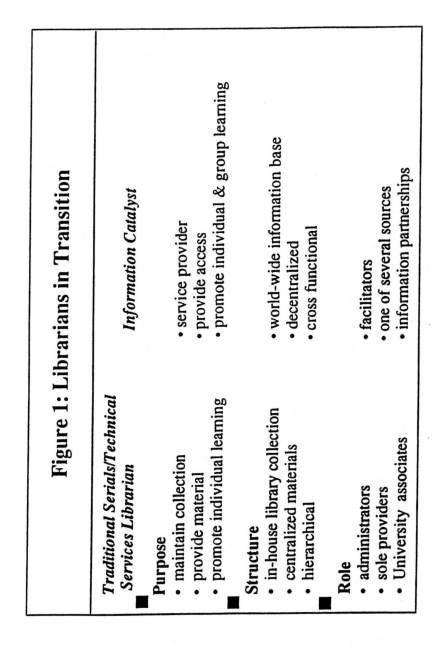

Figure 1: Librarians in Transition

Traditional Serials/Technical Services Librarian

■ **Purpose**
  - maintain collection
  - provide material
  - promote individual learning

■ **Structure**
  - in-house library collection
  - centralized materials
  - hierarchical

■ **Role**
  - administrators
  - sole providers
  - University associates

Information Catalyst

- service provider
- provide access
- promote individual & group learning

- world-wide information base
- decentralized
- cross functional

- facilitators
- one of several sources
- information partnerships

retail chains use Electronic Data Interchange (EDI) with their suppliers. EDI involves using standard data structures, a common data dictionary, and a highly structured standard syntax so that trading partners with incompatible computer systems can easily exchange data without human intervention. This "hand-in-glove" relationship saves the costs associated with re-keying or writing special programs to reformat data. In another partnership arrangement, IBM and Sears are forming a new information technology vendor and client partnership, where IBM will run a data network for both companies. This allows Sears to focus on its core retail business, and saves them from having to support the computer hardware and software involved in maintaining a network.[6] Even traditional rivals are forming partnerships. You only have to go as far as your bank's Automated Teller Machine (ATM). Traditional competitors are partnering in banking networks, using the same ATM network system to provide banking services to their clients.[7]

Partnerships provide a myriad of ways for independent organizations to provide more value and service. Opening new distribution channels, eliminating material or data inspection, providing new product or service capabilities, reducing inventory costs, and managing development risks are examples of opportunities to be exploited. Taco Bell, a fast food chain, serves as a concrete example. It determined that its value-added activities lay in the service provided by front-line employees with customer contact. It subsequently farmed out its food preparation operation. This allowed Taco Bell to focus on customer service, leaving the back room food preparation process to companies with scale and cost advantages.[8] Closer to home, some universities and publishers are partnering to provide "just-in-time" printing of textbooks, which reduces inventory and delivery costs for both parties, and improves delivery performance.[9]

Given the pressures of the library marketplace, the partnership theme will increase in terms of promise and necessity. Consequently, library management needs to continue to improve its ability to pursue and manage strategic partnerships.

PRINCIPLES OF PARTNERSHIPS

The successful partnerships described above do not occur without careful planning and attention to implementation. Just as in personal partnerships, business and service partnerships are not entered into lightly. Similarly, their success is based on specific principles that guide the actions of both parties.

Principle #1: Start TQM at Home and Share the News

To engage successfully in a partnership, potential partners should have some TQM efforts in place (e.g., as defined in the Baldrige requirements). Internal operations are usually easier to improve and control than external ones; therefore, it makes good sense to start improvement processes at home. In terms of broader TQM involvement, the larger player in the partnership should be willing to be a mentor for smaller partners and help assess their TQM progress.

Principle #2: Respect Your Partner's Position

Partners go through a negotiation process, which helps define their respective roles, constraints, needs, expectations, possibilities for adding value, and economic positions. This process implies give and take, where there is a healthy degree of compromise and a willingness to change for the overall gain. For example, to share serial publications pattern data, librarians need to accept standard volume and issue labels, which are consistent within the database but may not reflect the library's "traditional" practice. This change is incurred in favor of lower transaction costs, faster cycle times, superior quality, and new capabilities.

Principle #3: Look for Seamless Connectivity

Libraries must have better connectivity options from their suppliers for partnerships to be successful. "Seamless connectivity" means that one partner provides compatible electronic data to another for automated processing, so labor and delivery costs are eliminated or largely reduced. Libraries need the ability to exchange business management data electronically with publishers, banks and service providers, as well as exchange serials collection management information with other libraries and Integrated Library Systems (ILS) vendors, using EDI and MARC standards. This allows, for example, a library to transmit a claim electronically to an agent, and the agent's computer system to process it without manual intervention (i.e., manual sorting, routing, reviews, data entry, decision making, etc.).

Principle #4: Manage the Partnership by Fact

Partners should be able to demonstrate collectively the benefits sought in partnership, in terms of quality, productivity, economic benefit, return on investment, and strategic staying power. Partners should gauge the degree of mutual interest, shared problems, and ability to effect positive change. Each should win from the relationship. Potential partners should share mutual benefits, have a common vision, and concur to a large degree on projected results and how they will be measured. Once a partnership is formed, performance data on quality, throughput, cost, savings and responsiveness are necessary to spot problems and improve the reliability of the relationship.

Principle #5: Use Trust to Your Advantage

Partners must demonstrate mutual respect for each other. Although this does not mean sharing trade secrets, it does reflect the understanding that information will be shared. The successful relationships are not developed for the sole benefit of one partner. Partners must be able to trust one another's integrity and honesty. They must trust each other's commitment, starting at the top and permeating throughout each organization, to service quality and improvement. Finally, they must also trust each other's expertise in areas such as data quality and adherence to standard practices and data structures.

These aspects of trust must be nurtured by facts. Trust, however, may also require some leap of faith and cultural shifts based on new systems and structures. For example, as libraries begin to share serials check-in data and lists of available serials, they must trust the data and operational standards for the group as a whole to achieve economies of scale. Consequently, partnership means letting go of an "us versus them" perspective, and beginning to think of the parties in terms of "we."

Principle #6: Employ Patience and Perseverance

In addition to trust, partners must exercise patience and perseverance. Problems that are technically and organizationally complex take much longer to solve. In fact, empirical studies have shown that the time it takes to cut a defect in half (that is, from the existing defect level to the theoretical minimum) is between eighteen and twenty-four months, depending on the technical complexity and the number of entities involved in the solution. Reducing the number of claims, for example, involves several entities such as the reader, the library, the subscription agent, and the publishers, encompassing a variety of technical and regulatory issues pertaining to EDI and so on. These types of problems also require use of new management and planning tools and re-engineering techniques. They also require choosing from a range of potential trading partners and focusing on those with similar goals. By contrast, internal partners or associates can expect to cut defects in half in shorter time frames, typically six to twelve months. For example, a team of library staff and facilities/maintenance workers should expect to reduce energy losses by applying systematic problem solving methods and tools. Uni-functional teams on the other hand should turn the improvement wheel quickly (one to three months) since the data and solution are within their power (e.g., reducing check-in time or cataloging errors).[10]

DEFINING AND MEASURING QUALITY PARTNERSHIPS

While principles are important conditions for effective partnerships, forging new partnerships and exploiting new opportunities require re-thinking what services are offered and how those services are delivered. Whether they call it "process redesign" or "re-engineering," the players in the knowledge management business must take a fresh look at service creation and service delivery processes. Typically, this task begins with a map of the service delivery system.

Like travellers heading out on a new journey, librarians need a map of their business–a clear picture of how work gets done today and how it *could be accomplished more effectively and efficiently*. One such mapping technique is called Service System Mapping[sm]. This technique helps to explain the service delivery system from the client's or user's perspective–whether that customer is the end user or a distribution channel. Maps also help to focus attention on the internal flow of work right back to suppliers. With a holistic picture of how services are developed and delivered, maps can be used to streamline operations.[11] Implicit in streamlined operations are quality partnerships, clearly defined and measured. The following example illustrates a sample partnership.

Together We Stand . . .

Libraries, agents, and publishers are currently plagued by a collective inability to provide serials and other materials to end users in a reliable fashion. Instead of counting on materials to arrive on time, every time, end users (and consequently others in the service delivery chain) toil within a murky environment where materials too often do not arrive as expected.

The common vehicle used to fix the system once it breaks (e.g., a journal issue does not arrive when expected) is a "claim." The claim usually passes from the library through the subscription agent to the publisher, and back through the chain again. This is an expensive process for the service provider and a source of frustration to the library's customers. Claims do not prevent problems; they merely address service failures, thereby wasting precious resources and testing end user patience. Moreover, claims often create follow-up claims, and the problem worsens.

The claim problem is large and complex; thousands of end users, libraries, and publishers generate, process, and respond to millions of claims. Small alterations or improvements are not good enough. Large re-engineering efforts are needed. The good news is that within this lose-lose-lose environment there is the potential to achieve win-win-win situations by re-engineering this service recovery process.

Re-Engineering: A Thumb-Nail Sketch

The focus of re-engineering is to tackle system-wide problems. This involves looking at an existing process from start to finish, asking what is the purpose of the business process, and questioning the prevailing wisdom of the way work gets done. Productivity breakthroughs come through eliminating unnecessary steps and by streamlining the essential steps from the clients' points of view. These typically involve simplifying the work flow and then selectively using technology to make further improvements. Re-engineering also tends to represent large investments and implementation efforts. The following seven steps provide a useful roadmap.

Step 1: Form a re-engineering team
Step 2: Know your customer's current and future requirements
Step 3: Map and review your current service delivery system
Step 4: Measure the capabilities of the current service delivery system
Step 5: Set aggressive improvement goals
Step 6: Re-engineer the system to improve service delivery
Step 7: Solidify strategic partnerships

Step 1: Form a Re-Engineering Team

The first step in the re-engineering process is to form a team. The team should include individuals who know or can learn how the entire operation functions, who understand and are dedicated to customer needs, and who can pursue dramatic change in the name of improvement. The organization then must support that team by publicly committing to the results they seek, the methods they use, and the progress they make.

Step 2: Know Your Customer's Current and Future Requirements

Determine what elements of service, quality, responsiveness, and cost matter the most to your "customers." Use structured techniques such as Voice of the Customer (VOC) and Quality Functional Deployment (QFD). VOC is a process used to identify customers' needs, clearly understand them, and carefully translate them into service requirements. QFD is a structured system for designing projects and services based on VOC requirements.

Step 3: Map and Review Your Current Service Delivery System

Using techniques such as Service System Mapping^{sm}, flow chart your *current* delivery system. Separate this map into "bands." The top band represents the end user. Key "partners" in the service delivery chain are shown in the other bands. Focus your attention on the top band to understand how your clients experience your service. Also, the map should show, from left to right, the different phases of the services' "life cycle." Once you have created a map and gone through several revisions, review it with others in your organization to test for accuracy.

Figure 2 depicts a sample work flow for the claiming process. In the top band, libraries record the arrival of journals or "check them in." Claims are transmitted electronically (in e-mail) to a subscriptions vendor, where many are printed, sorted several times, and routed to Service Representatives. Service Representatives process these reports into another system, screening premature or other invalid claims. Valid claims are then printed and mailed to publishers, who screen and process them.

This delivery system has several weaknesses. First, it is not "predictive"; instead of issuing claims based on the expected publication date of an issue, the system simply waits a standard amount of time before generating a claim. Moreover, many claims cannot be automatically exchanged between library, agent, and publisher systems, but are manually "inspected" several times. This introduces unnecessary costs (e.g., manual labor, human judgement, increased cycle times, mail and printing, etc.). Problems are difficult to ascertain, as there is no automated way to spot abnormal claim volumes or check-in patterns.

Figure 2: Sample Claims Process

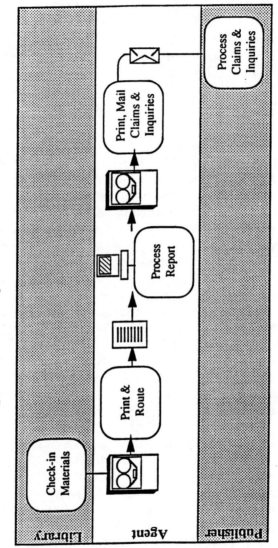

Step 4: Measure the Capabilities
of the Current Service Delivery System

Once the current process is mapped, step back and view it from the user's perspective. Asking the following questions can help get at key issues in the service delivery system:

- Who are the customers of the service?
- What benefits does the service provide for the customer?
- How can the intangible aspects of the service be made more tangible?
- How does the customer define quality service?
- Where are opportunities to improve the service delivery?

One way of getting the organization to focus on the client is to establish critical performance measures of quality and responsiveness. Also, look at ways to improve the process and eliminate waste. As part of this step, determine the key root causes of the service delivery system's failures, including those related to your partner's processes. Utilize this data as a baseline from which to re-engineer how work gets done.

Step 5: Set Aggressive Improvement Goals

Aggressive goals spur creativity. Without them, organizations routinely settle for much less than the collective talent of the staff can deliver.

Step 6: Re-Engineer the System to Improve Service Delivery

As you begin the redesign effort, some of the key design criteria that should be taken into consideration include:

- Identify the "moments of truth"; that is, identify any interaction between you and your clients in which they can assess the value of the relationship. Repeat this process for your suppliers.
- Simplify, integrate, and if necessary, automate. Ask what is the purpose of the task and why you are doing it. Eliminate those

activities which hinder or prevent achievement of the task, or which are not truly necessary to achieve it. Look for and eliminate duplicate steps that may be carried out in multiple departments or even within one flow. Eliminate hand-offs that result in backlogs or cause service delays or communication problems. Focus on those processes and tasks which *must* occur to deliver effective and efficient customer service. As Peter Drucker says, "in defining the task, concentrating work on the task, and defining performance, one can become more productive without working harder or longer."[12]

- Use structured information system development techniques, such as data modelling and work breakdown structures, to avoid the inefficiencies caused by duplicate data in your system. Information systems should produce results for the client, not just the service provider. Focus on your client's needs and expectations, and find ways to meet and exceed them.
- Manage a balanced profile of performance. Ensure that quality, delivery, cycle time and waste measures are captured in the process and fed back routinely to the service developers and providers.
- Look for opportunities to create or re-create strategic partnerships. Ultimately, you want to look at your entire service delivery system. Therefore, you must include key suppliers in your analysis.

Figure 3 represents an example of the re-engineered work flow illustrated in Figure 2. The task is to provide end users with accurate information on which journals have arrived at the library, where they are located, which issues are behind publication schedule or are not available, and which ones are, in fact, missing.

To accomplish this task more effectively and efficiently, libraries could partner with other libraries and share collection information. For example, libraries using Faxon Manager™ (a serials management system) automatically generate and transmit claims based upon publication schedules gathered from publishers and actual dispatch data. The system automatically loads the data, screens invalid claims without human inspection or intervention using normalized data structures, and spots problems which are re-

Figure 3: Re-engineered Claims Process

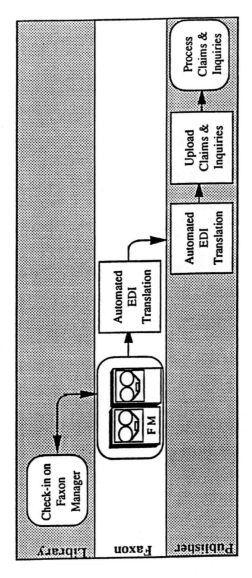

151

searched by Faxon staff. This process also eliminates the costs of unnecessary routing and sorting. The information is provided back to libraries for end users (shown by the double arrow) to prevent future claims, enable accurate status communication to the library's customers, and allow users to determine the journal's location in the library. Throughput and quality are enhanced between the agent and publisher, as valid claims are transmitted via EDI and loaded into publisher systems.

In this example, "re-engineered" relationships emerge. Partners no longer inspect incoming claim data. All partners invest in standardizing data interchange using EDI. Libraries augment their focus on helping end users access data, and spend less time claiming and inspecting. Agents focus on providing data interchange expertise and on spotting problems for immediate corrective action. Publishers, protected from a deluge of invalid claims, focus on rapid delivery of issues.

Step 7: Solidify Strategic Partnerships

Based upon the re-engineered flows, identify and measure "moments of truth" in the partnership. For example, in the event of a service delivery failure, the following scorecard measures the effectiveness of an agent's or vendor's performance on claims processing (Figure 4):

Measures provide critical feedback for continuous improvement and go hand-in-hand with the Service System Map in zeroing in on improvement opportunities.

CONCLUSIONS

TQM is an emerging catalyst in the quest for more efficient and effective knowledge processing. At its nucleus, TQM is a structured system for meeting and exceeding client/user needs and expectations through organization-wide participation in the planning and implementation of service *breakthroughs* and continuous improvement process. Breakthroughs in service delivery come through challenging the prevailing wisdom, tackling system-wide weak-

Figure 4: Scorecard for Vendor Claim Processing

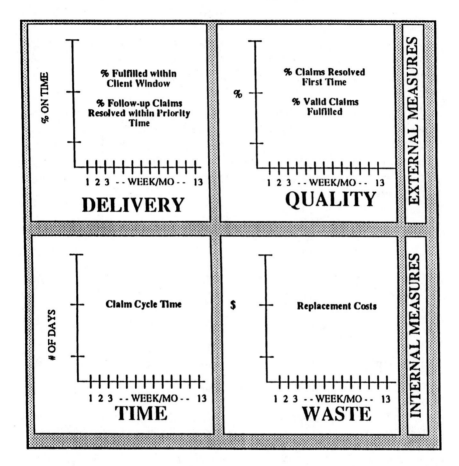

nesses in service delivery, and involving not just the library director and staff but authors, patrons, university colleagues, vendors, and publishers.

The kinds of "quality partnerships" described in this article have several implications for the library community. Librarians must continue to take a more market-driven and customer-focused view of their work. As librarians and information specialists know all too well, the "market" is a moving target. The ability to react quickly to change becomes the driving force for the need to establish solid partnerships. Librarians, therefore, need to designate staff whose function it is to identify, initiate, maintain and improve internal and external partnerships. Consequently, librarians will need to master a host of quality tools and communication skills, and to take a fresh look at their traditional work. This requires looking beyond traditional relationships and players in order to respond to new customer demands.

Finally, as a consequence of seamless connectivity and emerging standards, librarians must be willing to let go of the ownership of information and trust their partners. Librarians can then focus on continually improving their core competencies in service, access and facilitation, and develop new services as technologies and markets change.

NOTES

1. Mary Sieminski Anderson and Christina Bellinger, "Funding and the Future of the Academic Library: ACRL/NEC's Twentieth Anniversary Conference March 26-27, 1992," *ACRL New England Chapter News* 65 (Summer 1992): 5.

2. Janice F. Sieburth, "ACRL National Conference: Academic Libraries Achieving Excellence in Higher Education," *ACRL New England Chapter News* 65 (Summer 1992): 2.

3. Natalie Hall, "A Match Made Online: Two Service Providers at UCLA Plan to Wed Form and Function in the 1990s," *American Libraries* 21 (January 1990): 70.

4. Bruce Flanders, "NREN: the Big Issues Aren't Technical," *American Libraries* 22 (June 1991): 572, 574.

5. Julie Nicklin, "Rising Costs and Dwindling Budgets Force Libraries to Make Damaging Cuts in Collections and Services," *Chronicle of Higher Education* 38 (February 19, 1992): A28.

6. Laurence Hooper, "IBM and Sears Data Networks Seen Merging," *Wall Street Journal* 220 (August 18, 1992): A3,A6.

7. Benn R. Konsynski and F. Warren McFarlan, "Information Partnerships—Shared Data, Shared Scale," *Harvard Business Review* 68 (September-October 1990): 114-120.

8. Leonard A. Schlesinger and James L. Heskett, "The Service-Driven Company," *Harvard Business Review* 69 (September-October 1991): 71-81.

9. Richard N. Katz and Richard P. West, "Sustaining Excellence in the 21st Century: a Vision and Strategies for College and University Administration," *CAUSE Professional Paper Series* 8 (1992): 1-21.

10. Arthur M. Schneiderman, "Setting Quality Goals," *Quality Progress* 21 (April 1988): 51-57.

11. Service System Mapping is Service Mark of GrayoJudsonoHoward, Cambridge, MA. For more information about mapping and its use in developing performance measures, see: Richard L. Lynch and Kelvin F. Cross, *Measure Up! Yardsticks for Continuous Improvement* (Blackwell Business, 1991, Cambridge, MA).

12. Peter F. Drucker, "The New Productivity Challenge," *Harvard Business Review* 69 (November-December 1991): 77.

LEARNING FROM THE EXPERIENCE OF OTHERS

Total Quality Management Initiatives in Higher Education

Maureen Sullivan
Jack A. Siggins

INTRODUCTION

An article on Total Quality Management (TQM) in the U.S. News and World Report's 1992 edition of *America's Best Colleges* begins with this statement:

> In their search for economic salvation, America's troubled academic institutions are turning to a ninety-two-year-old guru

Maureen Sullivan is an Organizational Development Consultant under contract to the Association of Research Libraries Office of Management Services. Jack A. Siggins is an independent Management Consultant.

[Haworth co-indexing entry note]: "Total Quality Management Initiatives in Higher Education." Sullivan, Maureen, and Jack A. Siggins. Co-published simultaneously in the *Journal of Library Administration,* (The Haworth Press, Inc.) Vol. 18, No. 1/2, 1993, pp. 157-169; and: *Integrating Total Quality Management in a Library Setting* (ed: Susan Jurow, and Susan B. Barnard), The Haworth Press, Inc., 1993, pp. 157-169. Multiple copies of this article/chapter may be purchased from The Haworth Document Delivery Center. Call 1-800-3-HAWORTH (1-800-342-9678) between 9:00 - 5:00 (EST) and ask for DOCUMENT DELIVERY CENTER.

157

named W. Edwards Deming, whose management theory runs directly counter to the do-your-own-thing philosophy that has characterized the haphazard administration of most colleges and universities. Deming's ideas, referred to as "TQM"–for Total Quality Management–have become to this generation of college presidents what the "pursuit of excellence" was to their predecessors. Indeed, sixty-one percent of the 870 college presidents surveyed in the 1993 U.S. News poll say that their schools have adopted or are considering adopting TQM programs.[1]

Clearly, the Total Quality Management revolution has entered higher education in the United States. A number of experts and practitioners in the quality movement describe TQM as a journey, not a destination. The journey has begun in a number of colleges and universities and in many areas of academia. Faculty, administrators, deans, librarians, students and staff are actively engaged in various stages of TQM implementation. This article offers a general overview of TQM initiatives and programs in higher education.

In July 1992, more than five hundred participants attended the Third Annual Quality Symposium held in Pennsylvania's Lehigh Valley. The symposium's theme, Quality in Action in Academe, brought together a variety of individuals from government, business and education to explore ways to expand the use of the total quality process in all levels of education, from pre-school through graduate education. Provosts, deans, presidents, librarians and faculty attended from such institutions as the Universities of Michigan, Wisconsin, Maryland, Rhode Island, and Pennsylvania; North Carolina State University; Georgia Institute of Technology; Pennsylvania State University; American University; Lehigh University; Harvard University; and Oregon State University. Representatives from the U.S. Department of Education, the National Education Association, the Association of Research Libraries and the American Association for Higher Education joined in discussions of such issues as the role of TQM in the university, applying the TQM principles and processes to the administrative operations of a university, strategies for introducing quality concepts into the curriculum, and TQM as an approach to cultural change in the university.

The Second Annual Quality Symposium had been held the previous July at the University of Southern California. The 300 participants who attended that conference represented more than twice the number who had attended the first one at West Virginia University in the summer of 1990. The dramatic increase in the number of attendees at each subsequent symposium is another indicator of rapidly growing interest and involvement in TQM in education. Each year more institutions of higher education have been represented, the discussions of possible applications have been more extensive, there have been more reports of research in progress, and more experiences have been described.

TRENDS AFFECTING ACADEMIC INSTITUTIONS

At the Third Annual Quality Symposium, Dr. Marna Whittington, Executive Vice-President of the University of Pennsylvania, identified four revolutions which are confronting academic institutions and which are encouraging the use of TQM concepts to manage change:

The Communications Revolution

Technology has shrunk the globe and fundamentally changed the competitive and political environments. Computers have become so entrenched in our lives that none of our institutions could operate without them.

The Political Revolution

The fall of communism and the economic rise of Japan and Europe have dramatically changed the world.

The Revolution in Global Economics

The United States has moved from being the world's largest creditor to the world's largest debtor. At the same time, the erosion of our manufacturing base has decreased our ability to compete in the global marketplace, while damaging middle class wage earners and creating problems in distributing wealth.

The Quality Revolution

The quality movement in the United States has been spurred by the belated recognition of the positive impact of Dr. W. Edwards Deming's theories on Japanese industrial power. It is clear that American emphasis on mass production led to de-emphasis on product quality.[2]

TRENDS ENCOURAGING CHANGE IN ACADEMIC INSTITUTIONS

A confluence of several developments in recent years has created in many academic institutions a condition which is conducive to major changes in their strategies and operations. The principles and processes of Total Quality Management offer the most effective, comprehensive strategy for dealing with these changes.

Declining enrollments. Current trends indicate that enrollment in academic institutions is declining. Some predictions point to the reversal of this trend in another five years, while others suggest a continuation in the decline beyond five years. Whichever forecast comes true, declining enrollment over a significant period of time will be a major force for change.

Replacement of faculty. Articles appearing over the last few years in academic publications such as the *Chronicle of Higher Education*, as well as comments from individual faculty and administrators, reveal a growing concern about the problem of replacing retiring faculty with equally qualified scholars. The attraction of lucrative professions, such as business, law and medicine, makes it increasingly difficult for academic institutions to compete successfully for the most talented college graduates to enter teaching.

Rising costs. Costs associated with higher education are rising at a rate greater than the national rate of inflation. Expenses associated with running a university, especially those arising from salaries and benefits, are outpacing the ability to increase funding. Declines in federal and state support, resistance among parents to double-digit tuition increases, and the impact of the slumping national economy have hampered the ability to raise funds. Add to this the extra burden of the need for greater capital investment to replace deteriorating physical facilities and the fiscal prospects of many academic institutions become even bleaker.

Changes in enrollment. Competition for enrollment is also increasing among academic institutions in the United States. As the costs of obtaining a college education approach a level beyond the means of students and parents to pay, more people are seeking out those schools which not only fall within their constricted budget limitations but also provide more value for their dollars. The competition among graduate schools for students to fill their programs and help pay the salaries of faculty who teach in them is also heating up. Some observers also believe that in the near future, American institutions will be faced with significantly greater challenges from Europe and Japan, not only for foreign students but even for American graduate students. Already enrollments of international students in this country are declining.

Corporate education. Several corporations have made major investments in recent years to set up their own in-house programs to educate and train their staff, particularly managers. Major companies, such as General Electric, Westinghouse and Motorola, have taken steps to meet the educational needs of their employees and the companies themselves. Out of these efforts will likely come a desire on their part for a greater degree of collaboration with academic institutions. If colleges and universities are unable or unwilling to respond satisfactorily to this need, they may be faced with a growing challenge and competition from corporations to provide the education and training needed.

Work changes. Changes in the work being performed by staff brought on by the infusion of automation into all academic functions will continue to transform not only the flow of operations but also how individuals relate to each other. Pressure will increase to re-examine what and how work is being performed.

Greater accountability. As awareness of the challenges and changes described above has grown, interest in and demand for greater accountability have also risen in the academic community. Not only are administrators and others reassessing the allocation and expenditure of resources, but some faculty are also looking for ways to improve accountability in peer relationships, both within and outside their departments.

ORGANIZATIONS SUPPORTING TQM IN HIGHER EDUCATION

One aid in the process of introducing the concept of quality to an institution is the opportunity to learn from the experience of others who are also involved in TQM. In addition to insights based upon experience, a feeling of working together is gained. Several organizations have been developed to provide information and opportunities for institutions to share their insights and offer advice. They are having a major effect on the introduction of quality and Total Quality Management principles into higher education.

One of these is known as the National Education Quality Initiative (NEQI). This group was formed in 1988 by individuals in the U.S. Department of Education and the American Society for Quality Control. The organization attempts to span the entire educational experience in the United States and has three key objectives: (1) to include appropriate sections of quality science and associated arts into all courses in the United States from pre-school through graduate school and into continuing education; (2) to incorporate the quality sciences and the appropriate arts into all aspects of the administration and operation of all schools in the country; and (3) to improve the quality of the content and delivery of all material to students in the entire educational process.

Another organization is Project Equate, or simply EQUATE, which stands for Employee Quality Understanding And Teaching Excellence. The purpose of EQUATE is to promote opportunities primarily through conferences at the local and regional level for sharing success stories of quality improvement in education; to increase awareness of the value of quality improvement; and to identify sources of training and information for those who are engaged in quality improvement in education.

A third organization is GOAL/QPC. Their meeting in Boston in November 1991 brought together representatives from a variety of colleges and universities, as well as other educational institutions. GOAL/QPC's mission is "to be a leader in teaching Total Quality Management to organizations throughout the world." Through its research, publications and training programs, GOAL/QPC seeks to provide educators and administrators the means to learn more about TQM in education and ways to apply that learning. They have identified four main areas to accomplish that goal: (1) to create and increase opportunities for networking among the institutions and people who are involved; (2) to serve as a clearinghouse for information; (3) to develop a pilot GOAL/QPC Total Quality Management model that would be implemented in selected schools before being rolled out in others; (4) to develop a model process for implementation and written materials that would go with that process based upon the pilot experience in the selected schools.

The National Quality in Education Consortium was formed to address the needs of industry for education in Total Quality Management. The Consortium sponsors the annual "Quality in Academe" symposia to bring together representatives from government, industry and education.

In November 1991, college presidents in Pennsylvania met in Philadelphia with business leaders to discuss TQM. This meeting, called the Chief Executive's Forum for Business and Higher Education, was jointly sponsored by the Pennsylvania Association of Colleges and Universities and the Philadelphia Council for Excellence (PACE). PACE was organized by the Philadelphia Chamber of Commerce in 1983 to serve as a resource to organizations in the implementation of a total quality process.

Corporations also have provided important assistance to the effort to introduce TQM concepts into higher education. In 1992, IBM took a significant step, both to promote partnerships between business and academia and to encourage the application of TQM into higher education, by announcing that it would make major funding awards to eight colleges or universities. Through this program, IBM seeks to encourage the integration of TQM concepts into graduate, undergraduate and executive core courses in business and engineering programs; develop faculty research programs in

TQM; and apply TQM principles, concepts and methods to the operation of selected institutions. The hope is that the results will then be extended to other colleges and universities. Each award can be $1 million in cash, $3 million in IBM equipment, or some combination of dollars and equipment. These awards represent a significant investment in the development of programs to integrate TQM into institutions of higher education. After an extensive review of more than 200 proposals submitted, IBM Chairman John Akers announced the first award recipients on September 24, 1992. The nine institutions are: Clark Atlanta University and Southern College of Technology (a joint proposal); Georgia Institute of Technology; Oregon State University; Pennsylvania State University; Rochester Institute of Technology; University of Houston-Clear Lake; University of Maryland at College Park; and the University of Wisconsin.

Another example of cooperative effort between businesses and academia is "The TQM University Challenge." Five corporations–IBM, Milliken, Motorola, Xerox and Proctor and Gamble–are participating in this program which is designed to encourage the integration of TQM principles and concepts into the curricula of engineering and business schools, as well as into the administrative processes that support the development of those curricula. The program calls for each company to select one or two universities to participate in a week of on-site education about the practice of TQM. These participating universities are then expected to engage in certain critical activities during the next two years (1992-1994). Activities include: a comprehensive self-assessment to identify what processes need to be in place to ensure successful integration of TQM into the curricula; completion and implementation of a specific plan for the integration of TQM; and establishment of an ongoing process to review implementation and foster its application by other universities and companies. The sponsoring companies will work with the selected universities to help implement these objectives.

ROLE OF LEADERSHIP IN TQM

In TQM, the overriding goal is quality, but the philosophy is one that assumes cultural change. It is a process that requires a new vision. This vision must be articulated and then followed by a process of helping everyone in the institution understand, accept and develop a commitment to that vision. The first and most important requirement in the successful implementation of TQM is the total commitment of the leadership to improving quality, and to the process of getting members of the community to the point that improving quality is the motivation behind everything they do in the institution. This motivation must extend beyond the administration and staff to faculty, students and other constituents.

Ellen E. Chaffee, a leader in the effort to introduce TQM in higher education and Vice-Chancellor of Academic Affairs for the North Dakota University System, has full-time responsibility for introducing the principles of Total Quality Management in the state. In a talk delivered in 1990, she described her view of the importance of Total Quality Commitment (their version of TQM):

> The critical challenge of the 1990's is to change our ways so that we are what we stand for and we do what we are. Higher education, more than any other social institution, must not only teach what moral leadership means, but also show what moral leadership is. We must go far beyond "good enough if you pay enough" to a passionate, ceaseless commitment to improving quality, improving productivity and decreasing cost.[3]

In his inaugural address as President of the University of Rhode Island, Robert Carothers, a leader in the movement to integrate the principles of TQM in higher education, announced his plan to establish the Academy for Quality at the university. In an article in the January 18, 1992, issue of the *Providence Journal*, Carothers described the academy as "the primary vehicle for all members of the University's staff." He went on to say that "we will make it available to all public employees . . . so that the lessons of quality can help restore the people's faith in the competence and integrity of state government and help restore to all government employees their sense of pride in public service." In the first few months of his tenure, Carothers communicated his plan of action for quality improvement to faculty and staff. He also charged the faculty and

student senates to take a leadership role in the implementation of
the plan.

SOME CHALLENGES FACING HIGHER EDUCATION

A significant number of colleges and universities–perhaps as
high as eighty–have indicated their commitment to the quality improvement methodology described by Deming, Juran and others.
There remains, however, a vast coterie of institutions who seemingly either do not perceive a crisis in higher education in this country
or their institution, or if they do, are uncertain about how to address
the problem. Whereas many members of the business community in
the United States, faced with challenges to their survival, have
finally recognized the validity of Deming's advice, no such widespread response has occurred in higher education, despite the rising
number of alarms sounded and reform proposals presented in recent
years by respected critics and educators.

The mood of complacency present in most higher educational
institutions in this country is revealed in the failure of many to
confront fundamental problems. While the root causes of this failure are too numerous and complex to detail here, a brief discussion
of a few will illustrate the seriousness of the concerns.

The first of these is simple to identify and understand. In testimony before the Congress in 1989, Christopher Hart, a professor in the
Harvard Business School, stated: "For quality . . . there is as yet no
predetermined body of knowledge to be taught and there is a crying
need for organized course material."[4] Professor Hart was speaking
specifically about the inclusion of TQM material in organizational
behavior courses, but the same is true for other standard business
school courses (with the exception of operations management) at
both the master and bachelor degree levels. This perception was
confirmed by Professor Jose Eulogio Romero-Simpson of the University of Miami in 1991: "The emphasis on the external or the
internal customer, which is characteristic of the TQM philosophy,
was clearly missing. The enhancement of productivity through performance is seen as an end, rather than quality improvement for
ensuring customer satisfaction."[5] The lack of courses and course

material is an impediment to the dissemination and understanding of the concepts of TQM among the very individuals who will be faced in the future with the challenge of shifting from the old paradigms to more responsive ones in business, academia and other areas.

Another barrier is the attitude of university and college administrators toward the delivery of quality services. Recently, academic institutions have come under greater pressure to justify their priorities and methods of expending resources. Sometimes this pressure has come from state legislatures which are under stress themselves to meet growing needs in other state functions with a declining level of funding. Sometimes pressure has come from accrediting bodies. In other cases, it is the board of trustees or influential alumni donors who have applied pressure. In all instances, the major focus has been, "What are we getting for our investment?" Traditionally, academic institutions have tended to respond by pointing to endowment size, the number of famous faculty, test scores, or other incidental factors as measures of quality.

Another fundamental problem facing institutions of higher education is the need to overcome resistance among faculty to the concepts of TQM. Faculty resist the marketplace vocabulary, such as "customers" and "suppliers," used in TQM, claiming that it suggests that professors "sell" their knowledge to students for the "price" of tuition. But the resistance goes much deeper than the repugnance of terminology. It is derived from the deeply-held belief among faculty at most institutions that they are the best arbiters of what is good for the students and the universities. Henry Rosovsky, for eleven years Dean of the Faculty of Arts and Sciences at Harvard University, expressed this philosophy most succinctly when describing the role of students and other non-faculty groups in decision-making at the university:

> What these constituents lack—with the exception of some individual alumni—is expert knowledge about the primary mission of universities: teaching and research. . . . The individuals with expert knowledge are to be found almost entirely among the academic staff. . . . Final judgments on educational questions are best left in the hands of those with professional qualifications: academics who have experienced a lengthy period of

apprenticeship and have given evidence of performing high-quality work, in teaching and research, as judged by their peers on the basis of broad evidence.[6]

The problem with this attitude is that the needs of the "customer," i.e., the student, have suffered as faculty, in their scramble for tenure and promotion, have gradually turned away from the strenuous and less glamorous task of teaching to the more rewarding and profitable one of research and writing. Ernest Boyer, former Chancellor of the State University of New York and the U.S. Commissioner of Education, described the situation in his report for the Carnegie Foundation for the Advancement of Teaching:

> ... In the current climate, students all too often are the losers. ... In glossy brochures, they're assured that teaching is important, that a spirit of community pervades the campus, and that general education is the core of the undergraduate experience. But the reality is that on far too many campuses, teaching is not well rewarded and faculty who spend too much time counseling and advising students may diminish their prospects for tenure and promotion.[7]

In many institutions, emphasizing research and writing over teaching is one of many accepted prerogatives of faculty. Even in Japan faculty prerogatives are a major problem. Professor Masao Kogure, Japanese winner of the Deming Prize in 1951, has noted that, while Japanese professors love to teach and consult on TQM, no Japanese university is using it. He cited professorial autonomy as a key stumbling block.[8] Faculty resistance to both the concept of emphasizing quality instruction and the eroding of prerogatives may be the final and greatest challenge for university administrators and others eager to introduce the concepts of TQM to their institutions.

Somewhat belatedly, in the opinion of some critics, academic institutions are beginning to seek effective responses to the massive challenges which threaten their fundamental philosophy, reputation and, in some cases their very existence. While improvement in higher education is possible without Total Quality Management, many colleges and universities have come to realize that TQM offers an integrated, holistic approach to systemic change.

NOTES

1. Andrea Gabor, "Total Quality Management," *U.S. News and World Report's America's Best Colleges 1992*, p. 20.

2. Marna C. Whittington, "Remarks Before the Symposium on Quality in Action in Academe at Lehigh University," July 31, 1992.

3. Ellen C. Chaffee, "Quality: the Key to the Future," Keynote Address at the First General Session of the American Association of Colleges of Pharmacy, Salt Lake City, Utah, July 8, 1990. Published in the *American Journal of Pharmaceutical Education* (Winter 1990), p. 350.

4. Christopher Hart, "Testimony Before the Congressional Committee on Science, Space and Technology," April 20, 1992.

5. Jose Eulogio Romero-Simpson, "A Total Quality Management (TQM) Organizational Behavior Course," *Quality Quest in the Academic Process*, edited by John W. Harris and J. Mark Baggett, (Birmingham, Alabama: Samford University, 1992): pp. 79-93.

6. Henry Rosovsky, *The University: An Owner's Manual*, (New York: W.W. Norton, 1990): 270.

7. Ernest L. Boyer, *Scholarship Reconsidered: Priorities of the Professoriate*, Special Report of the Carnegie Foundation for the Advancement of Teaching, 1990, pp. xi-xii.

8. Ellen Chaffee, "Total Quality Management in Postsecondary Education," *North Dakota State Board of Higher Education Newsletter*, July 3, 1990.

Total Quality Management: The Federal Government Experience

Robyn C. Frank

INTRODUCTION

Amid reports in *Newsweek* (Mathews and Katel, 1992) and the *Wall Street Journal* (Fuchberg, 1992) about the demise or only the partial success of Total Quality Management (TQM) in the private sector, the Federal government continues to view TQM as an approach that can help solve governmental management problems. This article looks at the origins, benefits, and barriers to TQM implementation in the Federal government. While TQM is not a panacea, it has brought about dramatic changes for the better in many government agencies.

The Federal government is often accused of wasting taxpayers' money. A 1990 *Fortune* magazine survey (Kirkpatrick, 1990) of elected and appointed officials of both political parties, academics, and other experts, showed wide agreement on the need for fundamental reform in the Federal government. The suggested reforms are based heavily on the management philosophy of TQM and the restructuring that has been done in the private sector during the last decade.

Robyn C. Frank is Information Centers Branch Head, Public Services Division of the National Agricultural Library, Beltsville, MD.

[Haworth co-indexing entry note]: "Total Quality Management: The Federal Government Experience." Frank, Robyn C. Co-published simultaneously in the *Journal of Library Administration,* (The Haworth Press, Inc.) Vol. 18, No. 1/2, 1993, pp. 171-182; and: *Integrating Total Quality Management in a Library Setting* (ed: Susan Jurow, and Susan B. Barnard), The Haworth Press, Inc., 1993, pp. 171-182. Multiple copies of this article/chapter may be purchased from The Haworth Document Delivery Center. Call 1-800-3-HAWORTH (1-800-342-9678) between 9:00 - 5:00 (EST) and ask for DOCUMENT DELIVERY CENTER.

To paraphrase the *Gettysburg Address,* the government is of, by, and for the customer. Providing customer services has been a major function of most Federal government agencies. The Federal government serves the public in such various roles as: regulator, inspector, grantor, and information and assistance provider. The quality of that service has been uneven depending upon which office or person a customer contacts for service. According to a 1988 Gallup survey of American consumers that was sponsored by the American Society for Quality Service, only thirty percent think the Federal government is operated competently (Carr and Littman, 1990). "Good enough for government work" is still the stereotyped phrase depicting a government employee's work performance. Many experts have put the cost of poor quality at about 25 percent of all costs in the U.S. service industries (McKenna, 1992).

In the Federal government, as in the private sector, the motivating factor for adopting TQM was a question of survival. With continually shrinking resources, Federal managers are pressed to carry out their current missions more effectively. Also, from time to time, there are threats of "privatizing" various functions of the government. TQM can be seen as a way to help make the public sector more competitive, thus avoiding the need to privatize (Walters, 1992).

While resources are shrinking, the demand for quality government service is increasing. Global competitiveness, for example, impacts the Federal government as well as private companies. The Government plays an important role in assisting the private sector by working to reduce or eliminate the time and paperwork required to get approval on products and services to be bought and sold, both within the U.S. and in world markets.

THE FEDERAL "CORPORATE CULTURE"

First, let's take a look at the Federal environment. The Federal government is the largest employer in the United States. The total full-time Federal civilian work force number is 2.9 million, of which almost 1 million are in the Department of Defense. There are an additional 2.1 million military personnel.

The civilian work force is widely dispersed geographically.

Eighty-two percent work outside Washington, D.C. at more than 22,000 separate facilities. There are 147 separate and independent departments, agencies, and commissions.

According to the Federal Quality Institute, Federal agencies are managed in a top-down, hierarchical, bureaucratic mode and operate through highly structured administrative rules and procedures. As a result, management styles tend to be non-participative and rigid.

In short, the government is a huge conglomerate of activities and functions generally operating under inflexible and outdated management practices and principles. The objectives of the government-wide TQM effort are to break down the rigidity and excess structure of the government, and to devise ways to enlist the energies and talents of the work force to meet the challenges of the nation (Federal Quality Institute, 1991).

BENEFITS OF TQM

Carr and Littman see TQM as a win-win situation for everyone involved in government. "It's patriotic and represents streamlining, but it also represents an improvement to the image of public service, which is what everybody wants" (McKenna, 1991).

They also suggest that TQM offers everyone in government (elected or appointed officials, top career administrators, middle managers, and employees) tangible and intangible benefits (Carr and Littman, 1990).

Elected or appointed officials benefit from increased performance by agencies at lower cost. These cost savings can be used to add needed programs or to reduce deficits. In addition, a customer-oriented government greatly reduces the number of constituent complaints about government services. The officials can benefit in future elections by being credited with making government more efficient.

Top administrators can gain recognition by providing a vision of excellence and continuous improvement that is embraced by all staff. TQM allows him/her to cut waste from the program without reducing productivity and efficiency. It has also resulted in decreasing employee absenteeism and turnover.

A program of quality results in measurable savings both in time and money. For example, the U.S. Patent and Trademark Office reduced the processing time to record patent ownership from over 100 days processing time to 20 days, with a 50 percent reduction in errors. Employee suggestions at the Wright-Patterson Air Force Base (Ohio) resulted in a savings of $56 million in one year. At the Ogden Service Center of the Internal Revenue Service, recommendations from more than 50 Quality Improvement Teams improved customer service, realized savings and cost avoidance of over $3,730,000 (Fifth Annual National Conference on Federal Quality, 1992).

Besides tangible improvements in productivity and cost savings, TQM offers many intangible benefits. When the staff believe in the clearly defined mission of the agency, they believe that their work is very important (Gilbert, 1990).

Under TQM, the role of the middle manager changes dramatically. No longer are supervisors directing the staff but instead, they collaborate with staff on systems issues and improvement. More time is spent on cooperative efforts with other parts of the organization and in training, counseling, coaching, and mentoring staff. One of the greatest rewards for middle managers implementing TQM is in watching their employees grow and develop.

Employees experience the biggest changes in their role. They are challenged and empowered to create excellence. Self-managed work through teamwork, training, and delegated authority provides them with greater job satisfaction, motivation, loyalty to the organization, and pride in their work.

By seeking ideas from employees at all levels, agencies unleash untapped creativity, cut unnecessary processes, and enjoy productivity gains. Recently, the efforts of a self-directed work team, in the U.S. Department of Agriculture, resulted not only in improved morale and job satisfaction, but also an improved perception of their supervisors and a more positive outlook toward their agency as an employer. Staff are more enthusiastic, feel more respected, and believe that their professionalism has been enhanced (Travieso, 1992).

In a 1992 U.S. General Accounting Office (GAO) survey of government agencies, about 60 percent of respondents reported that TQM has enhanced organizational performance. Individual performance factors that were included were: (1) overall customer service, (2) customer satisfaction, and (3) cost reduction. The internal operating conditions studied included: (1) attention to customer requirements, (2) group process and problem solving skills, (3) internal communications throughout the organization, (4) change to a more participatory management, (5) timeliness of internal processes, and (6) efficiency. The GAO report stresses that organizational performance increases as the maturity of the TQM program increases (U.S. General Accounting Office, 1992).

EARLY EFFORTS WITH TQM

The Department of Defense (DOD) began a formal program of productivity improvement in the mid-1970s. These early programs were largely technique-driven and featured the prominent use of efficiency reviews, quality circles, and contracting. At the same time, DOD encouraged its contractors to analyze their processes to continuously improve the products and services supplied to the DOD. This program was gradually transformed into a TQM approach in 1987.

In 1988 the Secretary of Defense issued a DOD Posture Statement on Quality, which formalized the Department's commitment to TQM. As a result of DOD's early commitment to this effort, it remains one of the strongest proponents and provides among the best examples of TQM in the Federal government. Several DOD commands have received the President's Award for Quality and Productivity (similar to the Malcolm Baldrige National Quality Award for the private sector). In fact, General Charles C. McDonald, Commander of the Air Force Logistics Command, Wright-Patterson Air Force Base, in his acceptance speech in 1991 for the President's Award for Quality and Productivity, gave much of the credit of the Allies' success in Operations Desert Shield and Desert Storm to the implementation of TQM within DOD (McDonald, 1991).

GOVERNMENT-WIDE IMPLEMENTATION

The government-wide effort began as a Productivity Improvement Program (PIP) (a government-wide effort to improve the productivity, quality, and timeliness of government products and services) in 1986, under the direction of the Office of Management and Budget (OMB). Private-sector representatives urged the government to focus on quality improvement through TQM as the preferred approach to achieving both quality and productivity gains.

By mid-1988 the program had gradually evolved from the PIP program into a TQM effort. The Federal Quality Institute (FQI) was established in 1988 to be the primary source of information, training, and consulting services to agencies on TQM. Its three major functions were to provide quality awareness seminars and follow-up consultation to senior Federal managers; to develop and maintain a roster of qualified private-sector consultants; and to operate a Resource Center that would be a clearinghouse and referral source on information about TQM.

By 1990, the government-wide leadership functions and resources devoted to TQM implementation in OMB were consolidated into the FQI. At the same time, the responsibilities of the FQI were broadened, and additional resources were added to help it carry out its mission. It now offers direct "hands-on" advice and technical assistance to agencies to help them get started in the very early stages of TQM implementation. FQI also develops models of TQM to demonstrate to other government agencies; it has expanded its research and documentation of best practices and makes these results available to other agencies. The *Federal Government Total Quality Management Handbook,* issued by the FQI, became the document providing government-wide guidance for implementing TQM (Federal Quality Institute, 1991).

THE FQI INFORMATION NETWORK

The FQI maintains an Information Network on TQM applications and experiences, with an emphasis on Federal applications. The service includes a centralized database of case studies, essays, articles, and handbooks. The database is managed by the National Technical Information Service (NTIS), and is a part of the NTIS database, accessible on-line through commercial information service vendors such as DIALOG and BRS (Federal Quality Institute, 1992b).

FQI also provides access to the latest information through an electronic bulletin board service available to any Federal agency in the U.S. This system is intended to complement, not duplicate, the NTIS database holdings. The bulletin board provides six categories of information: (1) News items on Federal TQM efforts and innovations, (2) Looking for information (i.e., customer survey forms, Quality Council charters, etc.), (3) Upcoming TQM events, (4) New additions to the Federal TQM database, (5) Resource updates for local TQM information centers, and (6) Responses to requests for information (Federal Quality Institute, 1992a).

The Information Center, located at the FQI, provides referrals and basic information packages on TQM. Information Center staff is available to assist agencies in establishing their own local, regional, or field location TQM information centers. A *Guide for Establishing a TQM Information Center and Directory of Federal TQM Centers* contains a selected list of reference books, videotapes, journals, and newsletters that are useful as reference and teaching materials. A list of professional societies with information on TQM developments, as well as a directory of Federal TQM Centers, is included in the *Guide* (Federal Quality Institute, 1992c).

The FQI also maintains a list of private-sector contractors who have been competitively certified as qualified to assist Federal agencies in implementing TQM. Other services of FQI include: (1) providing one-day awareness seminars and other briefings to describe TQM to top-level government agency managers, and (2) providing direct assistance to agencies getting started, in such areas as establishing a quality council and drafting a quality council charter, a vision statement, and a TQM implementation plan.

FQI's training program focuses on three major principles: (1) Achieving customer satisfaction (both internal and external customers); (2) Involving everyone in the process; and (3) Making continuous improvement. The FQI has reformulated the TQM philosophy into seven elements. They are:

- Top Management Leadership and Support
- Strategic Planning
- Focus on the Customer
- Employee Training and Recognition

- Employee Empowerment and Teamwork
- Measurement and Analysis
- Quality Assurance

Of the seven elements, strategic planning is one of the most important. In many instances, however, the lack of long range planning has been a major hindrance to TQM implementation.

BARRIERS TO IMPLEMENTING TQM IN THE FEDERAL SECTOR

Although TQM is supposed to bring about positive change and a more efficient government, many agencies have held back from embracing and implementing its principles and methods. There are several reasons that TQM has not been implemented government-wide.

First, TQM is voluntary. Many managers are therefore not willing to commit the necessary time, resources, and training. Several private and Federal administrators now feel that in order for TQM to work throughout the government, the President must actively support it and make it mandatory. "Excellence in government is missing the most important ingredient: leadership" (McKenna, 1991).

Indeed, TQM represents a large expense of time–six to twelve years–and money. It is reported that on the average, up to 15 percent of a staff's time on a regular basis is spent on TQM (Walters, 1992). Training is expensive, especially when using outside consultants. Some agencies have taken a "training the trainer" approach in order to save costs (Shoop, 1991).

TQM requires long-range planning, which is difficult when operating on a one-year budget cycle. Add to that the fact that Congress and the Executive branch spend much time micromanaging and adding "pork" (funding for special projects within a Congressman's own state) to the budget process (Kirkpatrick, 1990). A multiyear budget cycle might be more conducive to long-range planning.

Also, with new administrations arriving in the Executive Branch, potentially every four years, planning necessarily becomes short term. Within agencies, the average time in office of a high appointed official is 18 months. Each time a new political appointee is selected, the priorities and initiatives of the agency are subject to change. The time of the learning curve for the new appointees takes months.

The Federal sector's lack of a clearly defined purpose also hampers TQM efforts. While private companies know that their mission is to make money, often government agencies have several different, and sometimes conflicting missions. Building a clear mission is a first step. Next, managers need to "weed out the bureaucratic underbrush that gets in the way of achieving it: rules and regulations, line-item budgets, procurement policies, and the like" (Osborne, 1992).

Another obstacle is that currently, there is no incentive for agencies to save money. If an agency cuts its costs, its budget is likely to be cut the following year. It has been suggested that staff share in the benefits of cost savings in a "gain sharing" incentive program (allowing all those involved in a quality improvement effort to share in its profits or savings) of cash awards or salary increases.

The Federal personnel system needs to be revamped and given much more flexibility in order to accommodate TQM. The current job classification and pay policies do not support a "flat" (non-hierarchial) organization. Several pilot programs are taking place to try different approaches to flexibility in personnel issues. For instance, at the National Institute of Standards and Technology (NIST), a new wide band pay scale replaced the rigid pay grades for its scientists and technicians. NIST also began awarding raises based on merit rather than time served. The extra pay cost is offset by not giving automatic raises to poor performers. This change in pay policy has made NIST much more competitive with universities and private industry in attracting and retaining highly qualified staff (Kirkpatrick, 1990). Another change that needs to take place is for quality to be incorporated into every Federal employee's performance standards.

Another important factor related to personnel policies is the role of middle management. Many middle managers feel that they are the most threatened by a "flat organization." There needs to be a way to best utilize their knowledge and skills without jeopardizing their standing in the organization. Possible roles for middle managers to play are as mentor, leader, trainer, counselor, and coach.

The GAO report identified nine problems that are moderate to major barriers to implementing TQM in the government. In descending order (from the largest to the smallest problem) the barriers are:

- Employees don't believe they are empowered
- Funding/budgeting constraints
- Employees lack information on TQM tools
- Resistance to participatory management
- Employee lack of information on TQM concepts
- Employee resistance to changing roles
- Federal personnel regulations
- Senior management unable to spend time
- Lack of long-term planning

A significant finding in this survey was that the respondents believed that the barriers decreased as their involvement in TQM increased (U.S. General Accounting Office, 1992).

OBSERVATIONS

There are many differences between the private and the public sectors. One of these main differences is that the private sector is competitive and the public sector holds a monopoly on its activities. TQM appears to work best in a manufacturing or a process environment. Streamlining a process such as acquiring and cataloging a book for a library collection, is a logical application of TQM. It is more challenging to apply TQM to the functions of formulating policy.

The GAO study revealed that about 68 percent of the Federal installations studied were involved in the implementation of TQM. The highest activity level was concentrated in the early phases. However, they reported that only about 13 percent of their employees were involved in TQM activities at the time of the survey. Although TQM is being initiated on a fairly wide scale, the depth of employee involvement is still thin. As the organizations mature in implementing TQM, and as they invest time and effort in the activities needed to carry on TQM initiatives, they find that the barriers become less difficult and they reap greater benefits (U.S. General Accounting Office, 1992).

TQM, however, cannot be regarded as a "quick fix." It takes time to successfully implement a total quality program with employee involvement and significant resources committed to it. Since politicians and political appointees often have a short term in Washington, they tend to look for short term results rather than long term improvement (McKenna, 1991). It takes a special type of leadership and commitment to make TQM work.

While many top administrators are wary of TQM, most of the good examples of TQM in operation, particularly in the civilian agencies, come from the field or within subunits of headquarters. Often smaller units can move more quickly and accomplish more. The grass roots approach to quality has often been blessed from on high, but not always fully supported. While this bottom-up approach is not the preferred way, it does build a solid foundation and momentum for future organizational change (Walters, 1992; Mizaur, 1992; Shoop, 1991).

It's important to keep in mind that TQM is not an end in itself, but rather, a tool to improve an organization and to satisfy its customers. It is a method to give new meaning to the phrase, "Good enough for government work."

SOURCES

Carr, David K. and Ian D. Littman. 1990. *Excellence in Government; Total Quality Management in the 1990s*. Arlington, VA: Coopers & Lybrand.

Federal Quality Institute. 1992a. Electronic Bulletin Board User Guide. *Federal Quality Institute's Information Network*. Washington, DC: Government Printing Office.

Federal Quality Institute. 1992b. Federal TQM Documents Catalog and Database User Guide. *Federal Quality Institute's Information Network*. Washington, DC: Government Printing Office.

Federal Quality Institute. 1992c. Guide for Establishing a TQM Information Center and Directory of Federal TQM Centers. *Federal Quality Institute's Information Network*. Washington, DC: Government Printing Office.

Federal Quality Institute. 1991. *Introduction to Total Quality Management in the Federal Government.* Federal Total Quality Management Handbook Series. Washington, DC: Government Printing Office.

Fifth Annual National Conference on Federal Quality. 1992. Awards Ceremony. Washington, DC. Awards Ceremony Program.

Fuchberg, Gilbert. 1992. "Total Quality" is Termed Only Partial Success. *Wall Street Journal* 210, no. 66 (October 2): B1,B9.

Gilbert, G. Ronald. 1990. Jump-Start Your Team for Quality. *Government Executive* 22, no. 11 (November): 54.

Jasper, Herbert N. 1992. Down the Quality Road. *Government Executive* 24, no. 4 (April): 37-40,60.

Kirkpatrick, David. 1990. It's Simply Not Working. *Fortune* 122, no. 13 (November 19): 178-180,182,186,190,194,196.

Mathews, Jay and Peter Katel. 1992. The Cost of Quality. *Newsweek* 120, no. 10 (September 7): 48-49.

McDonald, Charles C. 1991. Acceptance Speech upon receiving the President's Award for Quality. Washington, DC.

McKenna, Joseph F. 1991. TQ Government. *Industry Week.* 240, no. 21 (November 4): 12-14,18-19.

_____. 1992. Laying Siege to Washington (And OtherPoints Inefficient). *Industry Week* 241, no. 12 (June 15): 20-21.

Mizaur, Don G. 1992. Quality: Moving with Glacial Speed. *Government Executive* 24, no. 10 (October): 69.

Osborne, David. 1992. Why Total Quality Management is Only Half a Loaf. *Governing* 5 (August): 65.

Shoop, Tom. 1990. Can Quality Be Total? *Government Executive* 22, no. 3 (March): 20-21,23,25.

_____. 1991. Uphill Climb to Quality. *Government Executive* 23, no. 3 (March): 17-19.

Travieso, Charlotte. 1992. An Experiment with Self-Directed Work Teams. *Government Executive* 24, no. 5 (May): 42-43.

U.S. General Accounting Office. 1992. *Quality Management: Survey of Federal Organizations.* Washington, DC: Government Printing Office.

Walters, Jonathan. 1992. The Cult of Total Quality. *Governing* 5 (May): 38-43.

Total Quality Management in the Defense Fuel Supply Center: Issues and Observations

Eugene E. Matysek, Jr.

This article examines Total Quality Management (TQM) activities at the Defense Fuel Supply Center (DFSC) from the perspective of the criteria established by the Federal Quality Institute for the Quality Improvement Prototype (QIP) Award. This award was established to recognize successful adoption of TQM principles by federal organizations and to offer these organizations as models for the rest of government to aid in improving the quality, timeliness, and efficiency of services and products.1 The criteria elements for the award are:

1. Top Management Leadership and Support
2. Strategic Quality Planning
3. Customer Focus
4. Training and Recognition
5. Employee Empowerment and Teamwork
6. Measurement and Analysis

Eugene E. Matysek, Jr. (1950-1993) was an Operations Research Analyst with the Defense Fuel Supply Center, Cameron Station, Alexandria, VA.

[Haworth co-indexing entry note]: "Total Quality Management in the Defense Fuel Supply Center: Issues and Observations." Matysek, Eugene E. Jr. Co-published simultaneously in the *Journal of Library Administration,* (The Haworth Press, Inc.) Vol. 18, No. 1/2, 1993, pp. 183-190; and: *Integrating Total Quality Management in a Library Setting* (ed: Susan Jurow, and Susan B. Barnard), The Haworth Press, Inc., 1993, pp. 183-190. Multiple copies of this article/ chapter may be purchased from The Haworth Document Delivery Center. Call 1-800-3-HAWORTH (1-800-342-9678) between 9:00 - 5:00 (EST) and ask for DOCUMENT DELIVERY CENTER.

183

7. Quality Assurance

8. Quality and Productivity Improvement Results

Using these criteria as starting points this article addresses issues with which DFSC management expected to deal as the organization began using Total Quality principles, and examines some of the key on-going issues.

The Defense Fuel Supply Center, a primary level field activity of the Defense Logistics Agency located in Alexandria, Virginia, is charged with the mission of providing comprehensive energy support to the uniformed services and other federal agencies. The primary focus of the organization has always been the provision of fuels and energy products to a world-wide network of military customers.

After relatively unsuccessful, low-level efforts several years ago, DFSC's total quality efforts are only now beginning to take shape. The current activities and investments started in September of 1991.

TOP MANAGEMENT LEADERSHIP AND SUPPORT

This is an absolute. In a highly structured, monopolistic or bureaucratic organization, the cultural changes required for success in total quality cannot occur without the support and leadership of the senior executive. In the case of DFSC, efforts that started two years ago at the middle manager level floundered for lack of support from above. In September 1991, shortly after assuming command of the Center, the current commander hired a Special Assistant for TQM and made clear his support of and commitment to the TQM philosophy.

In addition to the senior executive, support of TQM activities must come from a majority of senior managers. In most federal organizations these managers are very pragmatic and are loathe to lend their support to any effort that cannot demonstrate mission value, either actually or potentially. They are also reluctant to surrender authority by empowering subordinates. In the DFSC case, the Special Assistant for TQM managed to demonstrate the value of the tools of Total Quality, thereby securing support from a majority of these senior managers.

DFSC created a TQM infrastructure based on the commander's model of management. In this model, senior management is responsible for strategic or long-range issues; middle management is responsible for operational, short-range issues; and first-line supervisors and their employees are responsible for tactical or immediate issues. The Total Quality infrastructure at DFSC consists of three organizations. The Executive Steering Council, which is composed of all of the senior managers and the senior staff of DFSC, meets on a weekly basis to review and guide the organization's priorities. The Process Review Groups are ad hoc groups of managers who are assembled to guide process improvements at the policy level. Process Action Teams are temporarily chartered working teams charged with formally examining a process critically with the goal of recommending improvements.

STRATEGIC QUALITY PLANNING

The TQM effort in DFSC has always been connected to the strategic planning process. As the center began the latest Total Quality efforts, the strategic planning process was the way the concepts, tools, and techniques of TQM were introduced to the managers. This provided the opportunity for them to see the concepts at work in a process they agreed was important to the organization, and allowed the Special Assistant for TQM to guide discussions of other potential applications of the tools and techniques.

The strategic planning model adopted by DFSC included: vision, mission, values, objectives, goals, and tasks. This model required input from the senior leadership of DFSC as organizational vision, mission, values, objectives, and goals were determined. The leaders were committed to ensuring that the resulting product became operationalized. The next level of the strategic plan, tasks, was created by teams of employees involved in appropriate aspects of the organization. This energized a portion of the work force to see the strategic plan as a living document closely connected to the day-to-day business. This connection becomes more emphatic as the resource manager and budget officer begin making budgetary decisions based on priorities established by the strategic plan.

CUSTOMER FOCUS

In the relatively insular world of the military petroleum community, customer focus has been a cultural value for years. Key military players rotate between assignments with their parent services and DFSC, maintaining contacts and familiarity with both systems. DFSC brought a panel of customers to the strategic planning conference and sought their input in support of the long-range planning efforts. Several initiatives among the tasks in the strategic plan aim at improving various aspects of the relationship among DFSC, its customers, and its suppliers.

In spite of this close customer relationship, DFSC discovered its perception of customer service was not without need of improvement. The customer service handbook is seriously out of date and actions have been initiated to update it.

TRAINING AND RECOGNITION

DFSC took a top-down, just-in-time approach to training for total quality. DFSC developed a range of classes for presentation to employees. Resource expenditure for the training program is considerable, including investment in teachers, training sites, travel expenses, and supplies.

The major training effort from September 1991 to March 1992 focused on training for the senior managers. This was to ensure they understood the principles and tools of TQ and could use them in their organizations. Presentation of this two-week course began in June 1992. The focus of the first week is on the principles of TQ, the tools available, teamwork concepts, and teaching techniques. The second week is given over to a practical exercise in which these supervisors form teams, attack a problem using the process improvement model, and brief their results and recommendations to the commander and senior managers. Virtually all of the recommendations made by these teams have been incorporated into the DFSC system. When the supervisors complete the training, they are encouraged to apply the concepts learned and to communicate those concepts to their subordinates (in recognition of their role as organizational "coaches"). Supervisory training is scheduled to be completed by December 1992.

Another class provides just-in-time training for members of Process Action Teams. The objective of this training is to communicate the key tools and techniques needed by the team members. Course outlines were also developed for introductory, familiarization, and refresher training for individuals and work groups.

The classes need to inform and inspire. Generally the personnel attending the classes have the perception of Total Quality as just one more in a long string of quality improvement programs, all defunct. All of the training sessions attempt to clearly communicate the level of commitment the DFSC leadership has to the TQM principles and to impress on the attendees that the tools and techniques are available to help them do their jobs, not as some additional step imposed on the organization.

Issues relating to recognition have been discussed inconclusively several times at Executive Steering Council meetings. Federal award and recognition programs and performance evaluation regulations provide the baseline from which these discussions proceeded.

EMPLOYEE EMPOWERMENT AND TEAMWORK

Results of employee involvement in the task writing portion of the strategic plan are encouraging. Team members are selected based on their level of involvement in a specific strategic planning goal. They are given general management guidance and then empowered to address the issues involved creatively. The analytic process the task-writing teams are taught allows each individual the opportunity for participation while guiding the team toward consensus.

Supervisors attending the two-week training course report their employees ask when and how they can get involved in TQ. To that end, the Center recently started a four-month test of a method for gathering employee recommendations for process improvements. This test, based on the feedback mechanism of Crawford Slips, is similar to Milliken's OFI (Opportunity for Improvement) forms. The Crawford Slip provides a means for team members to write their ideas in concise form on a slip of paper.[2] The OFI is an informal suggestion process used by Milliken and Company to capture employee ideas and provide quick response to those ideas. At DFSC, these ideas are referred to the appropriate office for action and answer. Status and responses are posted monthly in a public place. The concept has engendered some initial interest among the work force.

MEASUREMENT AND ANALYSIS

As the training program advances, the level of TQ awareness within the organization increases. The perception of the Executive Steering Council is that the next step is the creation of an inventory of major processes operational in the Center. The results of this inventory, although helpful in getting managers thinking about their business in terms of process, were determined to be clumsy and unusable. After some discussion a modified tack was recently started. The Executive Steering Council agreed to attempt to flow chart in detail the system by which the Center's most important product, bulk petroleum, is provided. This effort started with a macro-level flow chart of critical processes. The next step is the expansion of these generalized processes to sub-processes and even more detailed desk-top processes. When completed, the Center will be able to use these flow charts as the basis for identification of areas for measurement and improvement.

Additionally, as a result of their exposure to the tools of TQ, many of the managers are experimenting with various new measurement ideas in management reviews and internal briefings.

QUALITY ASSURANCE

DFSC had a well developed product quality assurance process prior to beginning the development of TQ culture. Internal quality assurance to ensure control of processes has been based on the Internal Management Control (IMC) program. As the measurement and analysis efforts go forward, DFSC plans to incorporate the IMC efforts with TQ efforts.

QUALITY AND PRODUCTIVITY IMPROVEMENT RESULTS

It is too soon in the cycle of improvement to judge what the results of the DFSC investment in cultural change will be. DFSC leadership expects a five year investment before the culture matures sufficiently for managers to see significant results. There is evidence of the beginnings of change, however.

After a year of weekly meetings the Executive Steering Council accepted ownership of the program and are more proactive in seeking improvements. They no longer indicate a preference for letting the Special Assistant make proposals; they are managing the Center's progress into the future.

A cadre of trained middle managers are educated and starting to use the TQ tools and techniques to assist them in doing their jobs. They are also charged with encouraging the spread of the culture throughout the organization. The success of the effort to improve quality, effectiveness, and efficiency of DFSC lies with the abilities of these leaders.

The organization began examining its operations in a systematic manner as a prelude to critical evaluation of its processes. Unlike efforts in the past, this effort is driven by a recognition of external customer requirements gleaned during face-to-face meetings with the senior management team and internal customer requirements based on system optimization.

The rank-and-file employees eagerly await opportunities for participation. The concepts of empowerment and customer service are clearly inspirational.

SUMMARY

To make Total Quality the operational management model in a Federal agency takes strong leadership support; a commitment to invest in both the technical and personnel issues through training; responsiveness to and knowledge of internal and external customers; and a commitment to tying these three together in a coherent, process-based strategic plan.

NOTES

1. Federal Quality Institute, *Quality Improvement Prototype Award, 1993 Application* (Washington, DC: U.S. Government Printing Office, 1992), pp. 1-6.

2. Janet Fiero, "The Crawford Slip Method," *Quality Progress* 25, May 1992, 40-41.

Index

Note: Page numbers in italics refer to illustrations; those followed by t refer to tables; and those followed by n refer to notes

Accountability, effects on higher
    education, 161-162
American Productivity and Quality
    Center, 11
American Society for Training and
    Development (ASTD), 11
Association for Quality and
    Participation (AQP), 11-12
Association of Research Libraries
    (ARL)
    TQM model of, 57-70,*62*
    evaluation of, 68-69
    expansion in, 68-69
    identifying products, services,
        and customers in, 65
    implementation of
        customers expectations and
            needs in, 63-66
        divisional planning in, 69
        exploration process in, 59-60
        guiding principles in, 64-65
        identification and
            measurement in, 66-67
        initial pilot project teams
            in, 67-68
        initial steps in, 59-61
        management commitment
            in, 60-61
        organizational assessment
            in, 61,63
    organizing for quality in,
        61-65,*62*

strategic planning in,
    61-65,69
team member skill
    development in, 68
vision in, 64-65
ATM. *See* Automated Teller Machine
Automated Teller Machine (ATM),
    partnership arrangements
    of, 141
Awards
    as an open door for others
        wanting to learn, 134
    Baldrige award,
        63,130-132,131t,132t
    benefits of, 132-134
    better service for customers from,
        134
    documentation of organization's
        efforts for, 133
    examples of "best practices" for,
        133-134
    objectives for, 133
    proposed action plan for, 134-135
    publicity for libraries from, 134
    rewards of, 132-134
    trained evaluators for, 133
    validation of current quality
        programs in libraries for, 133

Baldrige, Malcolm, 130
Baldrige award, 63,130-132,131t,
    132t

191